MAKE TIME YOUR SUPERHERO POWER!

G. Scott Graham
Lucie Hewitson, editor

True Azimuth Coaching

Copyright © 2016 G. Scott Graham

All rights reserved

The characters and events portrayed in this book are fictitious. Any similarity to real persons, living or dead, is coincidental and not intended by the author.

No part of this book may be reproduced, or stored in a retrieval system, or transmitted in any form or by any means, electronic, mechanical, photocopying, recording, or otherwise, without express written permission of the publisher.

ISBN-13: 9798548684875

Printed in the United States of America

CONTENTS

Title Page
Copyright
Introduction 1
Why I Wrote this Book 2
Twelve Chapters 4
Chapter One: Analyzing 7
Overview 8
3 Important Questions You Ought to Answer for Better Time Management ... 9
4 Essential Ways to Analyze Your Time 12
The Outsider's Point of View: How It Can Help Your Time Analysis ... 14
Top 4 Things You Need to Inspect In Time Analysis ... 17
What the Kaizen Philosophy Teaches Us About Time Management ... 19
Chapter Two: Attitudes 23
Overview 24
3 Surefire Ways You Can Achieve Better Self-Management ... 25
4 Ways You Can Improve Self-Discipline for Better Time Management ... 28
How Choosing to Live with No Regrets Can Improve Time Management ... 31

Self-Awareness vs. Habits: Battling Your Time-Wasting Habits	34
Chapter Three: Delegation	39
Overview	40
How to Utilize the Power of Delegation for Effective Team Time Management	41
Vertical Delegation vs. Horizontal Delegation: Which is Better?	44
3 Important Elements of Effective Delegation	47
The 8 Basic Levels of Authority in Delegation	50
7 Steps to Practice Effective Delegation	53
Chapter Four: Goals	57
Overview	58
How Successful Time Management Can Lead to a Great Life	59
Setting Goals: What are the Advantages for Time Management?	62
Moving Forward from SMART Goals to SMARTER Goals	65
Your Step-by-Step Guide to Setting and Monitoring Goals	68
Goal Setting and Goal Getting: Achieving Both for Success	71
Chapter Five: Interruptions	75
Overview	76
6 Steps to Handling Interruptions and Remaining Productive	77
8 Simple Ways to Manage Interruptions in the Workplace	80
How to Control Disruptive Urges While Working	83
Is Music an Interruption to Work?	86
Chapter Six: Meetings	89
Overview	90
3 Amazing Rewards of Effective Meeting Management	91

5 Ways to Boost Your Meeting Management Skills	93
Technology Advancement: How It Helps in Meeting Management	96
Top 10 Reasons Behind Wasteful Meetings	99
Chapter Seven: Planning	103
Overview	104
The 6 Traits of an Excellent Planner	105
How You Can Formulate a Work Plan and Time Plan	107
The Real Deal on Daily Plans vs. Weekly Plans	109
5 Common Schedule Disruptions That Can Ruin Your Weekly Plan	112
Chapter Eight: Priorities	117
Introduction	118
3 Essential Characteristics of Priorities That You Need to Learn	119
5 Important Benefits of Prioritizing	122
Urgent vs. Important: How to Set Your Priorities Straight	124
5 Tips to Help You Prioritize Better	127
The Pareto Principle: How It Can Help You Improve Time Management	130
Chapter Nine: Procrastination	135
Introduction	136
ProcrastiNation: An Enemy of Time Management	137
Conquering Procrastination: How to Plan and Implement Action	139
The 5-Step Plan to Battling Procrastination	142
The 6 Don'ts of the Fight Against Procrastination	144
Chapter Ten: Scheduling	149
Overview	150

Planning vs. Scheduling: What's the Difference?	151
4 Essential Tips to Help You Have an Efficient Schedule	153
The Great Benefits of Setting Appointments	155
3 Important Ways You Can Get an Early Start	158
How to Effectively Schedule Your Quiet Time	160
Chapter Eleven: Team Time	163
Overview	164
What is Accountability and Why Is It Important in Team Time Management?	165
6 Effective Ways to Improve Team Time Management	168
Utilizing a Team Time Log to Improve Team Time Management	171
7 Important Tips to Manage Time Wisely During a Meeting	174
Chapter Twelve: Written Communication	179
Overview	180
How Clutter Clouds Over Effective Communication in the Workplace	181
Written Communications: A Habit to be Corrected	184
4 Ways to Handle Your Written Communications at Work	187
How to Have a Cleaning Out Party	190
Conclusion	193
Your Superhero Power	194
About Scott Graham	197
Books by Scott Graham	199
Contact Scott Graham	201

INTRODUCTION

"The bad news is time flies. The good news is you're the pilot."

MICHAEL ALTSHULER

WHY I WROTE THIS BOOK

In my work as a career coach and business coach, one of the topics that seems to come up over and over is time management.

"I have trouble managing my time," I hear.

"What does that mean?" I inquire.

"I don't know. I just have trouble getting it all done."

That statement is as useless as an overweight person saying, "I have trouble with my weight." That describes nothing. Does that person have a desk job where they've been sitting in a chair for the past six years, slowly putting on weight? Do they eat too much pasta, pizza, and bagels and not enough vegetables? Do they snack between meals? Do they eat too many desserts? Or do they eat late at night?

Each of these questions – all other things being equal – pinpoints the real problem. "I have trouble with my weight" only describes a vague intention. It is difficult, if not impossible, to do something about a vague intention. However, once you have pinpointed a problem, then you can begin to work toward a solution. The person sitting at a desk all day can take walks on their lunch breaks. The person eating too many carbs can shift their meal choices. The person eating too many desserts can cut down on the sweets and find healthier alternatives.

Clearly, identifying the specific problem is the first step toward finding a lasting solution.

A few years ago, when I started a blog focused on time management., my hope was that I would help people evolve from, "I struggle with time management." to, "I have trouble with goals" or "I procrastinate" or "I need help with delegating."

Alas, the blog is now gone and I have moved on to other things.

One day I re-discovered my posts and as I read through them appreciated that they were still as applicable today as they were when they were originally written. So I have combined them into this book.

My hope is that after reading this book, you too will no longer say, "I have trouble managing my time." You will evolve, then solve, your time management issue.

G. Scott Graham
January 2017

TWELVE CHAPTERS

This book explores time management from twelve perspectives:
1. Analyzing
2. Attitude
3. Delegation
4. Goals
5. Interruptions
6. Meetings
7. Planning
8. Priorities
9. Procrastination
10. Scheduling
11. Team time
12. Written communication

I first learned about these various angles during my work as a distributor for Inscape Publishing. Now a part of Wiley and Sons, Inscape is the premier developer of the DiSC personality assessment as well as a number of other tools, including Time Mastery.

What I learned working with Inscape is that most people excel at most aspects of time management; they only need to improve in certain areas.

Figuring out where your real problem lies will help you to focus and direct your energy properly, resulting in better time management and overall success. Read on for an overview of the most important aspects of time management, as well as specific tips and strategies for improving in these areas.

G. SCOTT GRAHAM

CHAPTER ONE: ANALYZING

"We are what we repeatedly do. Excellence, then, is not an act, but a habit."

ARISTOTLE

OVERVIEW

In order to improve your time management skills, you must first reflect on your current habits. Before you attempt to cultivate a more effective and efficient approach to time management, it is critical that you take a step back and observe the way your time is currently spent on a day-to-day, moment-to-moment basis. Time analysis will help you to identify and improve your problem areas, as well as to locate and accentuate your unique strengths. Successful time management should be personalized; it cannot be implemented without a full understanding of your current habits and routines.

3 IMPORTANT QUESTIONS YOU OUGHT TO ANSWER FOR BETTER TIME MANAGEMENT

The development of good time management skills does not happen overnight. It is a long process that entails hard work and constant attention. Hence, you need to take it one step at a time in order to avoid feeling overwhelmed. The small successes will matter a lot.

One important part of the process is time analysis. To successfully reflect on your time management habits, you must ask yourself the 3 important questions below:

Who Controls my Time?
Do you know who actually controls your time? To find out, you need to analyze your time habits. Is it your supervisor in the office? Is it your parents? Or perhaps it's even your kids.

To learn the answer to this question, you need to keep a time log for two weeks or so and determine the patterns. The data here will point you to time habits that you have at the moment. You'll be able to clearly see which person or group seems to have control over how you use your time.

As a result, you can slowly move toward becoming the master of your own time instead of remaining a slave to others who may be manipulating you and your time.

What Are My Time-Wasters?
It's very common for people to have their own set of time-wasters. These are the things that drive you to use up a lot of time for not-so-important and not-so-urgent concerns. For example, are you the type of person who drops all your work when you're out with your friends? Do you tend to forget the hours that pass by when you're shopping or when you're on Facebook? These are a few of the common time-wasters that you can learn to keep in check.

From your time log, you can determine your own time-wasters. Why do you succumb to them? Analyze the answer to this question and you'll then know how you can avoid them easily in the future.

What Are My Productive Triggers?
Aside from discovering your time-wasters, you should also try to figure out your productive triggers. These are the things that motivate you to work harder and to stick to your plans and schedules. These also refer to the activities and habits that make you more productive and bring you closer to your goals.

One person may be driven to meet deadlines when working under pressure with a terror boss looking over their shoulder. On the contrary, another person may feel more inspired when working with an understanding and helpful boss in a fun and laid-back environment.

Indeed, in considering such an example, you come to realize that your productive triggers differ from those of others. Hence you need to determine your own if you're not yet aware of them.

In answering the 3 questions above and analyzing the implications of your answers, you'll definitely be able to evaluate your current time management skills and problem areas. Once you have accomplished this, the next step is to move forward. This can only be done by avoiding your time wasters, focusing on your productive triggers, and striving to master your own time.

4 ESSENTIAL WAYS TO ANALYZE YOUR TIME

Before you can even begin to improve the way you manage time, it's important that you document and understand your present use of time. Analyzing your day-to-day habits and activities can help you to build a larger picture of your current time management, and to answer this vital question: how can you make each day more productive and avoid chasing after the hours?

Record

The very first step you ought to take in the analysis of your time is to record everything you do each day. For a week or two, observe and make note of how you use your time. Keep a planner where you don't only write down your planned activities and tasks but also log what you actually did in a particular hour.

You need to be able to see the patterns of your time management at present before you can make adjustments or corrections. Thus, as much as possible, you should not skip any activity you carried out. Record everything and the amount of time you actually spent on each.

Review

Once you've got all the data in front of you, it's time to get down to business. Review and analyze which activities or tasks you spend more time on. Are they worth the time? Are these things important or maybe urgent but not really that important? Try to determine your time management patterns.

Also list down or check those that you believe should be given top priority and can affect other tasks. Perhaps there are also some things that you can combine to save time.

Retract

By this time, it should be clearer to you which things are taking up too much of your time. Perhaps you need to balance your priorities. Maybe you also need to pull back on the negative aspects that became clear through your analysis. For instance, if you used to spend 3 hours on the internet, you should exert extra effort to cut down on these hours, which you can then utilize for more important activities.

Write down all those time-wasters that you ought to minimize in order to have more time on your hands every single day for other essential matters.

Regulate

Now that you've completed the three steps described above, it's time to start regulating how you make use of your time. Be highly conscious of every hour and every minute each day. Catch yourself even before you fall victim to the temptations of time-wasting activities. Use an electronic planner with an alarm to remind you of what you should accomplish by the end of the day.

Regulate and monitor constantly. At first, it may seem too much work. But as you progress, you'll find that it becomes easier. Soon it will feel like second nature to you and you'll develop greater time management skills. Once you get there, you're going to love it so much that you won't ever want to slack off again and start from square one. After all, it's true what they say about how you can achieve the things that you used to just dream about once you've mastered time management.

THE OUTSIDER'S POINT OF VIEW: HOW IT CAN HELP YOUR TIME ANALYSIS

No matter how faithful you are to your time log and keeping record of all your activities, and no matter how efficient you are when it comes to analyzing the use of your time, there's still bound to be something lacking when you are your own subject of analysis.

Isn't it true that most people can't point out their own flaws? Isn't it true that at times, you can give great advice to others but cannot apply the same guidance to your own life? As in many other aspects of life, this is true when it comes to time management. Even if you truly focus and try to be objective, you'll still end up missing something. Hence, it's always better to get an outsider's point of view.

The Missing Links
Sometimes there are people who are in denial of the things they do wrong when it comes to time management. If you are one of these people, you may be skipping important links that will lead you to proper analysis and thus better time management habits.

You should therefore ask other people you work closely with – and trust – to tell you what you need to improve and how you can make better use of your time. You should also interview the people you live with because they may notice habits and tendencies that you are not aware of.

Going for Teamwork
Yes, you play a major role in your own time analysis. However, it's also crucial to ask those around you to give their views and provide assistance. Perhaps you can request your peers or colleagues to aid you in examining which steps you can combine or shorten and which tasks you can least prioritize. Maybe your family or teammates at work can also help you determine and remove the obstacles that are hindering you from becoming an effective time manager.

You have to welcome other people's suggestions so you can move further toward your goal of becoming more productive and mastering your own time.

Motivation from Others
At times, it's not enough that you get your motivation only from yourself. You may need to turn to others in your life to keep you going and struggling forward despite the many setbacks. Think of your huge "emotional why" that's often connected to loved ones.

It could be that your kids are the ones that inspire you to do your best. Then assess how you can use this motivation to help yourself in managing time better.

Outsiders can do wonders for your time analysis and for helping you achieve more effective time management. Just make sure to pick people who know you well. They should also be trusted individuals who care about you. Surely they will want to contribute to your goal through different approaches, such as collaboratively brainstorming tasks you should prioritize or minimize, and reminding you to stick to your goal at all times.

G. SCOTT GRAHAM

You can never have too many pairs of eyes checking in on you, or too many extra minds and hearts helping you along.

TOP 4 THINGS YOU NEED TO INSPECT IN TIME ANALYSIS

Analyzing your time is a necessity before you can even begin to plan how to improve your time management. It's something that you cannot skip and should take seriously. This will provide you with the data you need to evaluate your habits and create your very own personalized time management program.

Some people think time analysis is a piece of cake but it's not as simple as just keeping a time log. It takes so much more.

Below are the top 4 things you need to inspect and thoroughly consider when analyzing how you currently manage time:

Goals

In analyzing your time, you are required to keep a log of all your tasks and activities and how you spent the hours within a day. You can do this every day for about a week, or even an entire month. There is no limit; extend the time log as long as you need to in order to better assess your current management of time.

What many individuals fail to consider is the relationship between time spent and goals achieved. Upon reviewing your records, were you able to determine if the activities you did contributed to the achievement of your goals? Are you even aware of what your goals are in the first place? These are the things you must carefully analyze so you can move forward.

Activities

This is the main focus of time analysis. What do you do on a daily basis? What takes up most of your hours on weekdays and on weekends? It's a top priority to learn the specific activities that you engage in daily, weekly, and even monthly. It will help you to discover what you actually prioritize and what you consider a time-waster that should be minimized or eliminated.

Furthermore, you can also identify the productive activities that are more aligned with your goals and that helped you to focus your time and energy on future tasks connected to them.

Time Spent

The third important aspect that you must check out in time analysis is the time spent on each type of activity every time you engage in it. For example, what's the average number of hours that you spend on social media given that it's only for pleasure and not for business? Do you tend to spend more hours watching TV than doing actual work in the office?

In addition, it's of utmost importance that you determine which things you work so hard on and yet are ultimately not that important or significant to your goals. Sometimes there are tasks that take up much of your time but are not rewarding or will not benefit you in the long run. Analyze these too and make sure not to lose yourself in these anymore.

Recurring Problems

One last area to consider is the recurring problems that seem to arise. Are there difficulties that appear to repeat themselves as time passes? You must get to the bottom of these issues in order to avoid recurrence. Perhaps they stem from poor planning or lack of goal-setting. Whatever the reasons behind such obstacles, you have to discern their causes and effects so that you can move past them.

WHAT THE KAIZEN PHILOSOPHY TEACHES US ABOUT TIME MANAGEMENT

Have you ever heard of the Japanese Kaizen principle? This philosophy is often applied to various systems and certainly contributes to the improvement of time management in the long run.

What is the Kaizen Philosophy?
This philosophy began with the engineers of the Toyota manufacturing plant in Japan. It refers to continual incremental improvement in every part of a process or a system. When applied, every little improvement adds up to the overall success of the process or system.

Time Habits Change Over Time
The Kaizen principle emphasizes the significance of small improvements done continuously and consistently over time and in all parts or facets involved. Hence, if you apply this philosophy to time management, you will not change your time habits overnight, but will need patience and persistence to achieve meaningful change and success.

Analyze your past. Isn't it true that there were certain situations and influences in your life that helped develop the time habits you now possess? Because these habits were formed over many years, you cannot expect to change them instantaneously.

Once you have gained self-awareness and gathered knowledge about time management, you must slowly modify your time habits. What are the small things you can do to change your negative habits when it comes to handling time? Make sure to do these regularly, bit by bit.

Patience and Consistency are Essential
Of course it will take not only hours but perhaps months and even years to master effective time management. You need to be patient as well as consistent in your efforts. In applying the Kaizen philosophy, you have to make sure that every thing you do in each aspect of your life contributes to your improvement and to the achievement of your goals.

Daily habits are said to be highly influential to your success. This is because the practice of good daily habits undoubtedly falls under the Kaizen concept of applying small increments of change in every part of the whole and over a long period of time.

Education and Technology Play Major Roles
When you are trying to improve a system, it is crucial to keep educating yourself. In these modern times, it's also important to know which technologies can help make the system more efficient. In the case of time management, you have to keep researching new concepts and applications that you can utilize for your own good. You also have to pick out several technologies that will be beneficial for you such as electronic organizers and management software.

These are all important time management lessons that you can gather from the Kaizen philosophy. Such knowledge will aid you in your pursuit of better time management and balance in your life. This way you will understand the essence of taking small steps on a regular basis and practicing the daily habits that will take you closer to your goals every single day.

CHAPTER TWO: ATTITUDES

"For success, attitude is equally as important as ability."

WALTER SCOTT

OVERVIEW

It is impossible to acquire effective time management skills without first addressing the underlying attitudes and characteristics that define you and dictate your behavior. Time management is about logistics and planning, but it is also about self-reflection and self-awareness. Combined with the nitty gritty of schedules, goals and plans, identifying and improving your current attitudes will help you to achieve lasting progress.

3 SUREFIRE WAYS YOU CAN ACHIEVE BETTER SELF-MANAGEMENT

If you're the type of person who finds it hard to be punctual or tends to miss deadlines, it's probably high time you worked on your time management. These are clear-cut signs that you're not just weak in managing your time, but also in managing yourself.

Pursuing a more effective self-management will benefit you significantly. It will allow you to organize your tasks, balance the various aspects of your life, practice self-discipline and control, and much more. All of these practices will lead to a greater chance of realizing your dreams and improving your relationships, hence making you a lot happier – and more fulfilled.

Strengthening Your Willpower
The first method that you can employ in order to achieve better self-management is to strengthen your willpower.

Every single day, try something that you're not used to. This is one way that you can gradually improve your willpower.

Another technique you can go for is to anticipate all the possible barriers and setbacks in whatever you intend to take up or engage in. This way, you can prepare ahead of time. You won't be easily rattled by twists and turns along the way because you have a Plan B, a Plan C, and even a Plan D to back you up.

Developing Greater Self-Awareness

Bad habits can be difficult to break, and these can get in the way of effective and rewarding self-management. However, you don't have to waste a lot of time and effort trying to break such habits. What you can do is to improve your self-awareness instead.

Discover who you really are. Trace your history, family background, and experiences. Analyze all the different aspects of your personality and of your life. As a result, you'll become more aware of how your bad habits came to be, what fed them, and why you tend to fall into their trap over and over again.

When you are aware of your past, thoughts, feelings, actions, dreams, frustrations, and tendencies, you will be able to develop better control over them. At the same time, habits will cease to be automatic propensities but will become mindful choices. From here you can move further toward better self-management.

Formulating an Action Plan to Improve Your Habits

The third method that you should apply in trying to self-manage is to actually formulate an action plan to improve your habits. Of course it doesn't only stop at self-awareness, you have to have a clear action plan.

Firstly, you need to determine which habits you would like to change or eliminate. Self-awareness will help you pinpoint them while willpower will enable you to control them.

Next, you have to also think of a new and better habit that you wish to develop. This habit should make you improve self-management and bring you closer to your goals. Afterward, you should list all the steps you intend to take for a strong and bright start in attempting to develop this particular habit.

In this regard, you have to practice your newly acquired willpower and self-awareness, both of which will give you the consistency, purpose, and resolve not to go astray as you are working on your new habit. Therefore, you have to take note of specific actions that you can implement to prevent yourself from drifting.

Lastly, it's also important to note down the people who can help you in your action plan and what you believe will be their exact roles. Such knowledge should drive you to actually approach these individuals and ask for their help and guidance.

Here you will realize that the journey toward better time management and ultimately self-management in its entirety is not a solo flight. It also entails support from others, along with teamwork in terms of the organizations and groups you belong to.

4 WAYS YOU CAN IMPROVE SELF-DISCIPLINE FOR BETTER TIME MANAGEMENT

A lot of people complain about having so much to do but so little time in which to accomplish all their tasks. More often than not, the reality is that there is actually enough time for these things to be done. It's just that most individuals do not have the right attitude to manage their time in a prudent manner.

If you notice yourself frequently procrastinating, then you are probably in dire need of some redirection when it comes to time management. If you tend to always wonder where all those hours went at the end of a day, this is a clear-cut symptom of a lack of self-discipline. As such, it's about time you seriously worked on improving your self-discipline. This will truly do wonders for your time management, allowing you to accomplish all your tasks and even have time to spare for leisurely activities.

Take It One Step at a Time

If you attempt to implement a lot of changes all at the same time, you're bound to be overwhelmed. When this happens, you'll end up doing nothing at all.

You have to take it one step at a time. Why don't you start by focusing on just one goal that you have and listing down all the actions that you intend to take to work out this single goal? Carry out these actions one at a time and gradually move up to doing a few of them simultaneously.

Be sure to start small. Rather than forcing yourself to work for 6 straight hours in the office, you can break this up into 3 separate periods of 2 hours each. Then, as you master this, you can move on to having just one short break after 3 hours before working again for 3 hours.

Incorporate Action Plans into Your Lifestyle

Make sure to incorporate your action plans into your lifestyle so that they will be easier to carry out. For instance, if your work entails often dining out with clients, it will be difficult to stick to a diet that requires you to prepare home-cooked meals with specific ingredients. You should therefore just pick out restaurants that offer low-calorie and low-fat options to suit your weight reduction goal.

Identify Your Weaknesses to Overcome Them

Do you often end up browsing through Facebook for two hours when you check your notifications? Do you tend to set aside your tasks when you choose to hang out with your friends? Find out your weaknesses and identify each of them so that you can overcome them better.

If you know that Facebook will keep you preoccupied for a long time, make sure to check your notifications only when you have finished your to-do list for the day. Or if this seems too much for you, you can set the small goal of completing 3 tasks before logging into your Facebook account. Then set your cellphone alarm for just 10 minutes of Facebook browsing.

Chart Your Milestones and Reward Yourself.
Some people overlook the importance of milestones and rewards. Don't be too hard on yourself, or you might end up giving up. Chart your small successes and take note of the milestones. If you get to overcome your Facebook habit, that's already a great accomplishment. Reward yourself and continue. Once you get to focus on doing your reports in the office rather than gossiping with colleagues, that's another milestone too which you should celebrate.

Keep in mind that small successes and small celebrations will help motivate you and keep you going. Even if you do have some slip-ups from time to time, you just have to stay on track. Try not to feel defeated. Sooner or later, you'll reach your ultimate goal. And when you do, you'll discover just how amazing the journey has been for improving your self-discipline.

Conquering self-discipline is a momentous achievement that will benefit your time management. Work on this and you will surely be surprised to find that you've got more time on your hands than ever.

HOW CHOOSING TO LIVE WITH NO REGRETS CAN IMPROVE TIME MANAGEMENT

Numerous people find it difficult managing their time. A lot of them decide to work on improving it but end up failing in every attempt. Most of the time, it is because they have not been able to change their attitude.

If you want to be successful in the advancement of your time management, you have to start with your attitude. An essential part of this is learning how to live without regrets.

Being Positive
Think of a particular time in your life when you wished you had gone the other way, when you felt bad about a choice or decision. What happened afterward? What do you think would have occurred if you had no regrets whatsoever?

Perhaps if you had and still have no regrets in every aspect of your life, you would have a more positive attitude and outlook.

It would probably be easier for you to carry on with renewed strength and hope, with great excitement for what the future holds.

Regret can be short-lived if you wish it to be. Choosing to live with no regrets is a decision that can result in amazing things. Being positive, for one, and not dwelling on what had been or what could have been will do wonders in how you perceive things and will also influence how you speak, act, deal with problems, and relate to other people.

Improving Focus
Just picture yourself without any regrets. Wouldn't that be fantastic for improving your focus on the goals you intend to work on?

For instance, rather than sulking about the promotion that was not granted to you in the office and regretting the efforts you had exerted in the past, you can concentrate better on the big project assigned for you to lead. In accomplishing this project with flying colors, you ought to focus on how it will help the team and the clients instead of working hard just for a promotion. This way, you'll have more fun in the process, be able to achieve greater fulfillment in the end, and perhaps even be more appreciated and acknowledged.

Saving Time
Naturally, when there are no regrets hiding in any corner of your closet, you can be more focused, more confident, and more positive. All of these attributes will allow you to deal more effectively with the tasks you need to face at the moment. You can accomplish a lot more because your mind will be clear of negative "what-if" scenarios and "should-have-been" thoughts.

Moreover, without such regrets, you can feel happy and excited over the other good things in your life and also the blessings you anticipate in the future. Hence you will be more energized to do what you have to. The by-product is saving time. You will not waste any time pitying yourself and conjuring up thoughts of the horrible mistakes you committed.

Moving Forward

When you choose a life with no regrets, you get to move forward instead of finding yourself frozen in place. Think of all the times you could have been more productive rather than going through your work like a spaced-out zombie because of your regrets. Think of all the relationships you could have protected from pain and failure. Think of all the time you could have saved and used up for much better things. Indeed improving your attitude by not succumbing to the feelings of remorse, anguish, and self-pity will help you save time in the long run. As a result, you'll get to live a more gratifying life.

SELF-AWARENESS VS. HABITS: BATTLING YOUR TIME-WASTING HABITS

When you are young, you get to develop habits that naturally come about from the lifestyle your parents have brought you up in. Most of the time, you tend to absorb the same habits that your parents or other housemates have.

As you grow older, you discover that some of these habits actually contribute a lot to waste of time. They stand in the way of your goals and dreams, but it's just so difficult to brush them off and change them. What should you do to improve your time management despite these hindrances?

What are Habits?
Habits can be defined as attitudes or behaviors which are practiced regularly even without consciousness. These are tendencies that may be quite difficult to give up.

If you have several time-wasting habits such as watching TV, surfing the internet, talking on the phone, and window shopping, you will be faced with a huge challenge when it comes to managing time wisely.

How Can You Overcome These Time-Wasting Habits?
Don't fret. Habits may seem impossible to break, but there are ways to battle the bad ones.

The first and most important step to fight and overcome time-wasting habits is to make sure that you are aware of each and every one of them. Self-awareness and acceptance go together. This combination is the key to achieving better time management.

How do you even begin to develop self-awareness?
Keep in mind that developing self-awareness cannot be done overnight, not even within a week or a month. It's an ongoing lifelong growth. But of course, there are ways for you to get a headstart now while you can. The earlier, the better.

Starting right now, make it a point to be more aware of your choices and actions every single day. List the things that make you forget and forego tasks you need to finish.

Get to the root of these habits you have. Where and when did they start? Go back to the past and explore the people and situations that have influenced you to develop such habits. This will help you grow much more in self-awareness not only when it comes to time management issues but also in all the other aspects of your life.

In addition, be wary of the triggers of your habits. For example, if you know that going online will make you lose track of the time and end up wasting plenty of hours, you should hold off until after you have completed all your tasks. Definitely avoid feeding your bad habits, which you can only do by being 100% aware of the habits themselves and of their triggers.

Keep in mind that being aware will also enable you to replace your bad habits with good ones. Then you can focus on practicing the good ones on a daily basis so that they can eventually overthrow the negative habits you have.

In conclusion, you ought to know that habits are very, very hard to break. Thus, the solution is to boost self-awareness so that you can catch yourself before you even go there.

MAKE TIME YOUR SUPERHERO POWER!

G. SCOTT GRAHAM

CHAPTER THREE: DELEGATION

"The first rule of management is delegation. Don't try and do everything yourself because you can't."

ANTHEA TURNER

OVERVIEW

The path to efficient time management can't be traveled alone. Many people succumb to the impulse to take on too many tasks and responsibilities, simply because they know themselves to be capable of producing optimal results. While this thinking makes sense, it can also be a detriment, because it results in hectic, stressful work days and tight deadlines. Learning to delegate tasks to other members of your team is a crucial component of time management. Assigning responsibilities to others based on their strengths will save you time and allow you to focus on the bigger picture, leading to less stress – and better results – in the long run.

HOW TO UTILIZE THE POWER OF DELEGATION FOR EFFECTIVE TEAM TIME MANAGEMENT

Being a leader is not about hogging all the tasks that need to be done and thereby taking all the credit in the end. It's actually more about knowing how to delegate tasks properly and oversee everything from an eagle's point of view in order to attain the objective of a project. It's also about dealing with people effectively so that they don't feel as if you're swamping them unfairly with work or giving them more than they can handle.

When you're a leader, you should be able to use the power of delegation to your advantage. This is certainly not about showing off your amazing skills and talents and proving that you are the best. You've already done that. This is why you're leading the team.

Now you need to let others shine because whatever each member achieves and whatever the entire team accomplishes will reflect back on you. If you want honor and recognition, manage your team time wisely through delegation. As a result, you can accomplish more and to a higher quality.

More People, More Time
Just imagine how much time you can actually save when you have more people working at the same time. If you have a lot of tasks to do in order to complete a project, it can be done within a shorter period of time if you're able to delegate well. This means that you ought to distribute the assignments evenly as much as possible so everyone can make good use of the limited time available.

Determining Strengths, Discovering Skills
When delegating tasks, you should not just focus on the quantity but also the quality. Instead of giving out 5 tasks each, you need to analyze how long a particular task may take and who is the best person for this job. This way, you can make the most of your team time by picking people who can finish specific tasks more quickly but with better results. It is therefore of utmost importance to determine the strengths of your people and to discover each one's skills and abilities. Such knowledge will guide you in the delegation of tasks.

In some cases, though, you also have to push others to work on certain competences that you believe they possess but have not yet fully developed. When you see potential, encourage the person in that direction by giving the appropriate assignment. In this manner, you'll have more people doing a multitude of jobs with excellence.

Analyzing Tasks, Assigning Time
A good leader must be able to pinpoint all the big and small tasks within a project. You need to perform delegation analysis not only by getting to know your people better but also by studying the tasks involved too.

In analyzing tasks, you have to sort them according to the ones that you can and cannot delegate as well as the ones you're uncertain about delegating. Of course you cannot delegate everything, because there are some jobs that you yourself have to do. One example is being accountable for providing solutions to big concerns that may arise.

However, the ones that you can delegate should be matched with the abilities of the team members for maximum efficiency and time management. Meanwhile, the ones you are not sure about should be examined and evaluated individually. For instance, coordinating with other departments may fall in this indefinite category. In such a situation, there is no permanent decision or solution. You can elect your approach on a case-by-case basis.

When you utilize the power of delegation by following the above-described methods, you can surely improve your team time management. After all, delegation is known to make up a lion's share of time management when it comes to any form of group work.

VERTICAL DELEGATION VS. HORIZONTAL DELEGATION: WHICH IS BETTER?

In the corporate world and in any organization, delegation is viewed as an essential element of effective leadership and management. No matter how great you are at what you do, you have very limited time - 24 hours at most which you also have to use up for eating, sleeping, traveling, and spending time with your loved ones. Hence, you cannot accomplish much if you work by yourself only.

Traditional Delegation
In the traditional sense, delegation means passing on tasks down the line. This is what's commonly known as vertical delegation. If you are the team leader, for instance, you can only assign work to your subordinates but not to the other team leaders in the department.

This type of delegation goes a long way back and is still widely practiced today. It's effective not because of a shared sense of responsibility but out of obligation only. After all, an employee does not have any choice but to accept the task being assigned because it is his job. This is why some believe that such delegation does not bring about high quality of results. What's more, it can create greater feelings of resentment and bitterness especially toward those in authority.

Modern Delegation
During these modern times, many organizations are beginning to apply horizontal delegation. It is said to be more effectual because there is sincere teamwork and a shared sense of accountability for the goals targeted.

Several managers in a department, for example, can discuss the specific tasks that have to be completed and then go about dividing them among themselves. In this regard, they are all giving their agreement and commitment to working together to achieve a common objective. They are not applying any authority over one another.

In the same way, ordinary employees belonging in one team can discuss a project and assign tasks to one another according to what they have agreed on. The division of tasks can be according to ability, seniority, and/or schedule. Doing this will help them develop better responsibility, coordination, and cooperation in the long run while avoiding negative feelings toward superiors.

Certainly, it seems easier and faster to just apply vertical delegation at all times. However, you need to take into consideration what will be more beneficial in the long haul. From experience, plenty of departments, companies, and institutions believe that horizontal delegation is better. Of course you must also take note that the two types of delegation can be combined and should be utilized based on the nature of the project undertaken or goal being pursued.

Before putting these two types of delegation into practice, you may also want to consult the people involved and ask for their views and opinions. This way, even if you will be applying vertical delegation, it will be more acceptable because it has been discussed. When being open about such things, you'll be surprised to see how much happier and more productive everyone turns out to be.

3 IMPORTANT ELEMENTS OF EFFECTIVE DELEGATION

Delegation can be tricky. You may be led to believe that you are delegating tasks effectively because your subordinates just say yes to everything you assign to them and deliver their results on time. But are they happy about it? Are you 100% sure that they will want to keep on following you without any say?

In most cases, employees get burned out and suddenly quit. Perhaps you have been passing on too much work that they could not handle. Maybe you were not fair in the distribution of tasks. There are many different reasons that you may not be able to verify because these people are mere followers but not participants in the project.

At times too, it is the one in the position of authority who ends up throwing in the towel because he cannot handle the work anymore. This is an indication that he was not able to delegate successfully, or perhaps did not even delegate in the first place.

So what are the important elements that ought to be present for effective delegation?

Humility

The first element is humility. This is on the part of the delegator who should admit to himself and to others that he will not be able to achieve a lot all by himself. He should believe in the ability of others too and be humble enough to allow others to help and be recognized and honored as well.

If you feel as if you're the only one good enough to do the work and if you never attempt to work out the training of new leaders, then you will always have a hard time moving up. You can never go places if you are alone. Thus, you must practice humility first and foremost.

Trust

There should always be trust between the superior and his subordinates, and among colleagues and managers. This is essential for delegation to be effective. The delegator must trust the delegatee enough to hand over an assignment, especially an important or crucial one. At the same time, it's also vital that the delegatee trusts the delegator so he will not feel used or abused but will be happy about the given assignment.

Remember, though, that trust is earned. You need to therefore build trust in your relationship with your colleagues, superiors, and subordinates. After all, this will also benefit you in the long run and make things easier at work.

Acceptance

The third element that must be present for delegation to be effective is acceptance. When it comes to delegating tasks, the delegatee must accept the delegator's authority. In this light, you must realize that you only have as much authority as the other person is willing to grant or accept. Indeed, this plays a huge role in making sure that delegation occurs smoothly and will not cause any hard feelings or stain any relationship.

What you have to take note of is that acceptance, just like trust, is earned. It actually goes hand-in-hand with trust so you need to also develop and enhance relationships continuously so that you can reap the benefits of effective delegation and be a better manager and team member.

THE 8 BASIC LEVELS OF AUTHORITY IN DELEGATION

A lot of managers and superiors make the common mistake of delegating without planning. Even more commit the error of delegating without determining and clarifying the level of authority involved. Many times they don't even understand what the different levels of authority are and how to apply them in various situations and to different people. Familiarize yourself with the 8 basic levels of authority so that the next time you delegate, you can apply one of these and lessen the confusion and potential problems.

Level 1: Gathering of Facts
This has the lowest level of authority because a delegatee is expected to gather and present facts only but is not given power to decide. The delegator will be the one to make a decision on the matter.

Level 2: Showing of Alternatives
In this second level, the delegatee goes a little further by showing and suggesting alternatives from which the delegator can select.

Level 3: Recommending Alternatives

Being given the authority to recommend is one notch higher because you do not just suggest the options but can now pick one to endorse based on supportive documents and your own reasoning. In this level, you get to have a say in the matter but the decision remains with the delegator.

Level 4: Deciding then Waiting for Approval
At this level, the delegatee now has the power to decide. However, the decision does not necessarily translate to action. The delegator has to approve it first before it is applied.

Level 5: Deciding then Acting Unless Rejected
In some cases, there are people whose positions in a company do not change but the level of authority goes up when it comes to delegation. This is because they are now more trusted. At this particular level, a delegatee can now decide and act unless the delegator rejects this decision.

Level 6: Acting then Reporting Results
For some people especially those in the supervisory and managerial positions, they can now act directly when tasks are delegated to them. They just have to make sure that all results are reported. Naturally, they still have to practice caution and good decision-making before acting so as to provide excellent results they can be proud of.

Level 7: Acting then Reporting Only If Not Successful
At this level, the delegatee can also act straight away. But this time, he or she does not need to report all results but is only required to do so if the outcome is not successful. There are freelancers and field workers who are given this level of authority even if their positions are not considered managerial.

Level 8: Acting Without Reporting
When you are fully trusted and your ability, experience, and performance in the past show your competence, then you might be given this level of authority when tasks are delegated to you. Level 8 consists of acting without the need to report. Some company CEOs or presidents have this privilege, for example.

Now that you have learned these 8 fundamental levels of authority, it will be easier for you to identify which is sensible and practical for particular people and for specific situations. This knowledge will help you to become a more effective delegator.

7 STEPS TO PRACTICE EFFECTIVE DELEGATION

If you already understand the purpose and benefit of delegation, the next target is to learn how to effectively delegate. This is where problems begin to mushroom here and there, causing more problems to come about along the way.

Here are the 7 steps to achieving and practicing effective delegation:

Plan, plan, plan.
Never act before thinking and planning. Before delegating any tasks, you need to plan first or else you might end up delegating to the wrong person, assigning the same task to several people, giving unreasonable deadlines, and ending up with low quality results.

Planning will allow you to see the bigger picture and thus be able to determine which tasks have to be delegated, to whom, and when.

Clear up the responsibility and expected results.
You have to be upfront and clear about the responsibilities of delegatees. It's also important to clarify expected and intended results. This way, you and the person completing the assign-

ment will be on the same page and will be able to effectively problem-solve if issues do arise.

Choose the right person for the job.
It is crucial to choose the right person for every job. Always take into account a person's reliability, background, skills, abilities, and experience before assigning any task. For instance, you cannot delegate a very important task to someone new to the team who's still learning the ropes.

Determine the level of authority.
You should also determine what level of authority is appropriate for the situation. This means finding out which tasks should be given to colleagues and teammates and to subordinates or even to subordinates of subordinates.

Moreover, levels of authority refer to the actual setup of the delegation. Sometimes, superiors just assign without any consultation. There are also times when people can recommend alternatives but you still decide on the matter. In some cases, delegatees can act on their own and just report if necessary. This last scenario is usually applied in horizontal delegation.

The process of passing on the job and monitoring the progress will also be dependent on the level of authority.

Define how to monitor and control.
Furthermore, it's important to define how you intend to monitor the progress of people who are completing delegated tasks. Are you going to have regular meetings? Do you have checklists or reports they need to submit every now and then?

You should also be wary of how to keep control of the situation. If you are dealing with outsourced freelancers, for instance, it may be more difficult to have control over them. Hence you must place checkpoints such as applying mini deadlines.

Keep motivating people.
Along with delegating tasks properly and picking the right people, you should make sure to keep up a motivating environ-

ment. If not, even your best people may start to digress or show poor performance eventually.

There are many ways to create such an environment. Different forms of motivation work for different types of people, so you need to get to know them too.

Emphasize accountability.
Once you have done all the steps above, do not forget to emphasize to delegatees that they are accountable for the work that has been assigned to them. You must hold them accountable for effective delegation to take place with minimal problems.

Following these 7 simple steps will make you a better delegator. Mastering the process of delegation helps to create more effective leaders and managers.

CHAPTER FOUR: GOALS

"Setting goals is the first step in turning the invisible into the visible."

TONY ROBBINS

OVERVIEW

Goal-setting is one of the most important practices associated with time management. Developing specific goals, both short- and long-term, will allow you to direct your energy wisely and efficiently. What are you working toward? What do you wish to accomplish? Once you learn to allocate and utilize time in accordance with your goals, you will be well on your way to lasting progress and success.

HOW SUCCESSFUL TIME MANAGEMENT CAN LEAD TO A GREAT LIFE

One of the greatest hindrances along the path to living a great life is not being able to balance all of the key areas of your life. At times, there are career-driven individuals who tend to neglect their relationships and find themselves unhappy in the end. There are also those who are good at dividing their attention between work and family, but then overlook their own health in the process. It's a big challenge to be able to even out your time among the many different facets of life.

Balance is Key

Did you ever perceive time as an equivalent of life? If you delve deeper into this concept, you'll realize that there's really some truth in it. Time is life, because you use it up every single day for the different aspects of your life: family, career, health, financial stability, social life, leisure, and personal development. It serves as a basis for how you live your life; what you prioritize and spend time on will affect the turnout of your life.

Just imagine those who have two families to attend to, such as the parents that they have to care for and the spouse and children that they also have to support and spend time with. Further, what about the people who even juggle two or three jobs or have a small business on the side? What if they're also active in various organizations or they have taken up several hobbies all at the same time? In these situations, tremendous effort must be exerted in order to balance everything.

Balance is key in living a great and fulfilling life. Of course there will be moments or periods wherein you have to prioritize certain areas. Even so, you just need to make sure that you won't completely forget about the other things that are also important to you and would contribute to a better existence in the long run. When you've grown in the areas you give precedence to or once you've settled problems in these aspects, then you should divert your attention to the other areas that you may have deserted or ignored.

First Things First
When you are able to apply successful time management, you'll discover how great life can be! You can move forward in the various facets of your life and maintain wonderful relationships. You can try new things or engage in favorite activities. You'll surely be happy upon attaining the sought-after effective and fruitful skill of time management.

First things first, though. In order to achieve it, you need to begin with goals. You can't just drift from one area of your life to another, hoping for the best. You can't just dip your toes in relationships or ventures that you're not sure about, only to test the waters and waste time without a clear direction.

Having goals will lead you where you want to go. Set a few long-term goals by envisioning the future that you wish for yourself. From there, you can come up with smaller goals in the various areas of your life. When you've done this you can then divide or balance your time accordingly. You can also choose the activities that will help you move closer to your goal.

Set your goals and move with the end in mind. Sooner or later you'll find yourself living the life you've always dreamed of!

SETTING GOALS: WHAT ARE THE ADVANTAGES FOR TIME MANAGEMENT?

Developing remarkable time management skills can prove to be very beneficial in many aspects of your life. Thus, you ought to allot sufficient time and effort to the advancement of your ability to manage time wisely.

Some people tend to head straight toward the actions or particular activities that help in managing time, such as keeping an organizer and multi-tasking. What many fail to realize, though, is the importance of setting goals before taking any sort of action.

Yes, setting goals is crucial in the improvement of time management.

Providing Direction

Picture yourself driving your car without knowing your destination. How would you feel? Where would you end up? It's the same as working on any project without being aware of the objectives. You cannot achieve your desired result of better time management if you don't have clear, set goals.

Some may claim that the improvement of time management is the goal. However, goals ought to be SMART--- Specific, Measurable, Achievable, Realistic and Time-Bound. You need to formulate your goals with these traits in mind. For instance, the set goal "to submit paperwork on time in the office throughout the year" is a lot better and will truly provide you direction. This means you can plan accordingly and carry out specific actions based on this goal.

Reducing Stress
How can setting goals reduce stress? Think about it. Even before you start the ignition of your car, you already know where you're headed. When this is the case, you can prepare the things you need to bring along. You can load your vehicle with enough gas to reach your destination without any problem.

Since you can also anticipate potential problems you may encounter, such as a bumpy road you have to pass through, you will be ready to address them in a timely and thorough manner. You'll make sure to have your tires checked, hence avoiding the stress and hassle of causing damage to your tires, which might delay you or even lead to an accident.

The same goes for any venture you intend to undertake. When you have clear-cut goals to guide you along the way, you don't need to do plenty of "trial and error" attempts. There are numerous potholes you can avoid too, plus all of the strain and anxiety that accompanies an uncertain endeavor.

Increasing Positivity
Setting goals before you take any action will increase your positivity too. You will be more motivated because you can already picture the desired results. Because there is much less stress, things are more likely to be smooth sailing. When this happens, you get to develop a more positive mindset which will push you to work harder and which can also attract more positive things toward you.

Furthermore, when you are more positive, you're likely to influence others around you to have this brighter outlook. This way, if you are working together on something, then you'll surely inspire one another to do better.

Enabling Greater Results
Naturally, because of all of the advantages described above, you're bound to have faster and better results. When you know your destination, you can reach it within a shorter period of time. The drive will also be easier.

In time management, if your goal is to submit papers on time, you can focus on setting a number of hours each day to work on these needed documents instead of completing an assortment of action plans that lead to different aspects of time management. You will also be able to avoid sources of distraction while working in the office. You will attain your goal sooner and have a more brilliant outcome as well.

MOVING FORWARD FROM SMART GOALS TO SMARTER GOALS

Whenever you encounter the topic of goal-setting, you've probably heard of the importance of formulating SMART goals. However, do you truly understand what this acronym stands for and entails?

What's more, there are two other characteristics of goals that are essential to consider. Now here's where you move from SMART to SMARTER.

For you to fully understand the proper formulation of goals, you need to absorb and grasp what each attribute requires. An example is also depicted under each for your benefit.

S for Specific

Which one is more specific: "To improve how I manage my time" or "To come up with a checklist of things I need to do"?

Yes, you're correct! The second one is indeed more specific. When you have such precise objectives, you'll have an easier time planning the actions that will help you achieve them. You can leave out the not-so-relevant activities too.

M for Measurable

Taking the example above, you can make the goal measurable by writing "To come up with a checklist of 7 to 10 things I need to finish". When you put it this way, it will be simpler for you to gauge your success based on the measurement given: the number of things that you need to list.

This is an essential trait in formulating goals because it will enable you to clearly determine if you are actually attaining them. You'll also have a better idea of how much more effort you ought to exert if you do fall short of your goal.

A for Accountable
Imagine if you had a community of support around your goals. As few as two friends to support you and ask you how you are doing will increase your success markedly. Tell others about your goal. .

R for Realistic
Goals must be realistic. This basically has a similar meaning to the previous trait of being achievable. With regard to the given example, "To come up with a checklist of 3 to 5 things I need to finish" sounds realistic or feasible enough.

Remember that goals should be realistic or you might end up feeling frustrated. Don't push yourself too hard because then you might lose motivation and won't have little successes to re-energize you and keep you driven.

T for Timed
Goals have to be timed too. There should be a definite time frame rather than leaving the goal open-ended. This will increase your motivation and ensure that you won't slack off in working toward your aim.

To improve the given example, you can make it "To create a checklist every morning of 3 to 5 things I need to finish within the day". When it's written as such, you achieve a sense of urgency because there is a need to accomplish the goal every morning. Furthermore, this goal exhibits the requirement to come up with the things that you want to do just for the day and not for the week.

E for Exciting

When you have a SMARTER goal, the E stands for "Exciting". Wouldn't it compel you to be more focused and to strive harder if your goal is exciting?

"Exciting" can differ from one person to another. Hence, you must set your goals to be thrilling and stimulating for you. It's not enough that you are aware of what you can enjoy and benefit from when you achieve a certain goal. You must have it written down too! This way, it's easier to visualize something that will rouse you and keep you going in spite of difficulties.

For the given example, you can write it this way: "To come up with a checklist every morning of 3 to 5 things I need to finish within the day so I can have more time so play with my kids."

R for Rewarding

A SMARTER goal should also be rewarding. This means that it ought to be something that will fulfill you as a person and make you feel good when you achieve it.

In the example used, the prospect of being able to spend more time playing with the kids and bonding with them can truly be rewarding for a parent especially if you have been feeling guilty about not having enough time for them. Since you value your relationship with your children, then including this in your goal can truly be rewarding.

Now that you understand the benefits of incorporating all of these characteristics into your goals, you can start off on the right foot when diving into any project or mission. Begin by formulating and writing down your SMARTER goals to provide you with vision and direction.

YOUR STEP-BY-STEP GUIDE TO SETTING AND MONITORING GOALS

Goal-setting is sometimes overlooked when people work on a project or engage in an activity. There are also instances in which people do set goals, but do so incorrectly or incompletely. Other times there are people who set good goals but forget to return to them in order to monitor progress. There are also those who are not open to adjusting initial goals in accordance with how things turn out or evolve along the way. All of these scenarios only steer you along the wrong path, toward unsatisfactory results.

So how should you go about it the right way? Here's a step-by-step guide that will help you to set goals properly and monitor or check them as you go through the process of working to achieve them:

Envision Your Long-Term Goal.
Your vision is very, very important. How do you picture yourself in the future? What do you wish to happen? This will enable you to decide on your long-term goal. Write it down in your plan-

ner or in a notebook. Make sure to come up with a SMARTER goal, which should be Specific, Measurable, Achievable, Realistic, Timed, Exciting and Rewarding.

Break It Down Into Monthly, Weekly, and Daily Goals.
Once you have decided on your long-term goal, the next step is to break it down into what you want to achieve on a monthly, weekly, and daily basis. List it all like a checklist so that you can easily monitor your progress. Again, don't forget to make SMARTER goals.

List the Activities Under Each Goal.
Now you can write down the activities under each goal which you feel will move you toward your desired accomplishments. These specific activities must lead to attaining the daily goals, which will then lead you closer to weekly and monthly goals. Ultimately, everything should direct you toward the fulfillment of your long-term goal.

Indeed, all of your goals ought to be aligned so that the direction is clear and you are sure not to deviate from the pathway.

Monitor Your Progress Every Single Day.
You cannot just work and work on carrying out the activities you planned. It's important to monitor your progress -- not weekly, every other day, but every single day. This is crucial because you also have daily goals. It will also help you to modify your activities for the following day. For instance, if you were not able to complete one activity or realize a goal for the day, then perhaps you can carry it over to the next day.

Monitoring will also motivate you to keep at it even in the midst of challenges. This way you can also celebrate your little successes. You'll be fully aware of how far and how long you still have to go in order to get to your long-term goal.

In monitoring goals, use your listed goals and activities as a checklist. In doing this you might even think of new activities or goals that will be helpful. Or you may cross out those that you deem unnecessary. This is where being open to adjustment comes in. After all, the smaller goals you initially set can still be changed. What counts the most is that your new goals will lead you faster to a better outcome.

Goal setting is certainly vital not only in time management but in all types of undertakings, no matter what aspect of your life is involved.

GOAL SETTING AND GOAL GETTING: ACHIEVING BOTH FOR SUCCESS

Experts would say that, in order to be successful, it is important to have your goals in mind at all times. You have to begin by setting clear goals to guide your path.

A lot of individuals are able to set their goals but tend to drift away after a while. Often they get dejected or distracted. Although they were successful with goal-setting, they forgot to do the goal-getting.

Three Elements of Goal Setting

Vision

Every person has to have a vision of the future before being able to set clear and specific goals. This vision will be your guide in determining the actual targets you wish to aim for and to attain in the different aspects of your life.

Challenge

It's not really a goal if there is no challenge involved, so you must aim for something that you want which will take some work and will strengthen your skills in the process because of the desire to get to the finish line – despite the setbacks.

Time

Another vital element involved in goal-setting is time. Naturally, you need to set goals that are time-bound or else there is no pressure to push you into action. Moreover, time counts in planning for goals that are feasible or achievable.

Incorporate these elements into the goals that you set so you will be driven to triumph in the end and so your everyday actions will be guided accordingly.

Three Elements of Goal Getting

Plan

Once you have set your goals, the next step is to plan how you can move forward from where you are now to achieve these goals. This plan should include specific steps of action as well as deadlines. It will serve as your guide.

Action

A plan is of no use without the proper action. You need to take massive action to reach your goals. It doesn't have to be a huge step at the beginning, but what you need to ensure is the consistency of your action. It also doesn't have to be done fast, so long as you do not go astray from what you need and want to accomplish.

Flexibility

Even if you have the best plan and you follow it to the letter with the right actions, there will always be some unknown and unanticipated circumstances that can get in the way. Expect problems to arise along the way and be prepared for flexibility. You have to adjust to certain things and perhaps modify your actions and even your goals if necessary. You also need to keep an open mind and be ready to change paths at times just to get the same results you desire in the end.

With these three elements in place, it will surely be easier to attain your goals. Remember that goal-getting is intertwined with time management because it requires you to go through the process of working toward your goals. In this process, you need to manage time wisely so you can pull off your master plan.

G. SCOTT GRAHAM

CHAPTER FIVE: INTERRUPTIONS

"If I was thrown for a loop every time I was distracted, I could never get anything done."

JODI PICOULT

OVERVIEW

No matter how effectively you plan and schedule, there will be people and events that interfere and use up your time in unexpected ways. These interruptions are inevitable. Therefore, rather than attempting to eliminate them completely, you're better off learning to account for them and address them while staying on track. You can actively reduce some interruptions, like certain distracting activities and stimuli; however, other interruptions are out of your control. Learning to distinguish between the two and to allocate extra time for unexpected interruptions is an important time management skill.

6 STEPS TO HANDLING INTERRUPTIONS AND REMAINING PRODUCTIVE

Whether you're at home or in the office, there are bound to be different interruptions that will get in the way of your productivity. Interruptions can keep you from accomplishing everything you've planned for the day or the week. However, these things just can't be avoided. Hence, you need to learn how to handle them well and remain productive so that you can stay on track as you work toward your goals.

Accept Interruptions
The first thing you need to do is to accept that interruptions are part of your daily schedule or routine. Thus, instead of getting frustrated over them, especially during crunch time, it's better to acknowledge that these things do happen. If you focus on your irritation and succumb to panic, it is far more likely that you'll end up not achieving anything.

Analyze Disruptions

You must learn to analyze your disruptions before you can actually work out a plan to manage or control them. If you really want to manage your time properly, you must take the time to note the usual types of interruptions that make you pile up on backlog work, the people who frequently disrupt your work, and the common concerns that are often involved. Discovering the patterns will allow you to plan ahead and to have some sort of leeway or back-up plan ready when these things arise.

Control the Controllable

Once you've analyzed the interruptions, you ought to realize that there are several uncontrollable situations that will sometimes hinder your plans. What you have to focus on, though, are the controllable things. For instance, if there's an emergency in the workplace that you really need to attend to, do it. It's out of your control. However, if there's someone in the office who always chats you up, this you can do something about.

Handle Interludes in Clusters

You must also learn to handle the interruptions in clusters. After all, many of these interludes are part of your regular routine so you ought to be able to place them in groups to save time and effort. For instance, if you're always interrupted by email notifications, you can turn it off first and just check your email at a particular time. If you're always disturbed by colleagues who drop in to discuss problems encountered, you can set a certain schedule for a regular meeting with them.

Regulate Your Calls and Emails

Many individuals are commonly interrupted by phone calls and emails. Hence, you need to tone down or at least regulate these calls and email messages. This means that you must make sure that all those you entertain are purely business. Make sure that unimportant things will not get in the way of your tasks and activities.

Reduce Socializing

Even though socializing with workmates and even on the Internet is helpful in cheering you up or keeping you sane amid your work, it has the tendency to be addictive or to end up taking more time than necessary. Thus, you have to limit it. Set scheduled breaks within the day wherein you can go on Facebook or some other social media network or chat with the people around you. At least you won't lose momentum when you socialize in the midst of working on something.

With these 6 important steps, you'll surely be able to practice greater control of the usual interruptions that hamper your productivity.

8 SIMPLE WAYS TO MANAGE INTERRUPTIONS IN THE WORKPLACE

There will always be interruptions in the workplace, whether you like it or not. There's no point in getting upset over these things, especially if you're in the middle of something very important. Nevertheless, keep in mind that there are many ways in which you can somehow manage them while you're in the office so that you don't end up wasting a lot of time on mundane things.

Below are 8 simple ways in which you can manage such disruptions:

Rearrange office furniture.
It's essential to assemble the furniture in your workplace properly so that you don't face the door or the area where many people usually pass through. It would be good to include a large piece of furniture such as a cabinet to block your view from potential distractions and also to discourage people from disrupting you.

Avoid loud sounds as much as possible.

If you can put your phone on silent mode and turn off the notifications in your email as you work on the computer, then that would really do a lot to lessen the interruptions. If you can't, make sure to lower the volume of the ringers on your cell phone and office telephone as well as the sounds coming from your laptop or desktop computer.

Stand up when talking to someone.
One way that you can keep a conversation short is to stand up while talking to a colleague who dropped into your area. Or once you've finished discussing what's important, you can stand up to signal the ending of the dialogue. Even when you're on the phone, this is also effective because you feel more in control of the time that the talk will take.

Be straight to the point.
Of course, you have to make sure that you are always straight to the point when talking to somebody or having a meeting. Whether you're leading the conversation or facilitating the meeting or you are just the follower in the setup, it's important not to beat around the bush and insert unimportant anecdotes.

Avoid social media when you can.
When you're in the office, you need to avoid social media as much as you can because this has a great tendency to lure you into spending hours on unnecessary things. Facebook, Twitter, Instagram, LinkedIn, you name it: you need to avoid it unless it's required for what you have to accomplish.

Set an alarm for breaks.
One effective method to control your time during a break is to set an alarm. For instance, if you have a one-hour lunch break, you must set the alarm for an hour or even less if you need to finish something important. Make it a habit to go back to your work area as soon as the alarm goes off instead of getting carried away chatting with workmates or doing something else.

Plan for and implement quiet time.
Quiet time means scheduling several hours in a row wherein you

just focus on your work in a place where nobody can interrupt you. For example, you can stay in the library without your phone for a few hours.

Build interruptions in your schedule.
It's vital to schedule for interruptions too. This means you cannot fill up your entire calendar with tasks and activities. There should be enough allowance for possible interruptions that can delay your work.

HOW TO CONTROL DISRUPTIVE URGES WHILE WORKING

When you are working, do you sometimes feel the urge to check your email first or take a look at your Facebook notifications? Are there moments when you feel so lazy that you just want to have a chat with a colleague or spend the time shopping online? These are definitely disruptive urges that you'll regret later on when all your tasks pile up and you start missing deadlines.

Indeed, you must ensure that you are in control while working. This means not giving in to disruptive urges even when you are totally tempted.

Use a Checklist
Instead of putting up a picture of your family and friends on your work table, you ought to place a huge checklist where you can best see it. This must contain your to-do list for the day. Use a red crayon or marker to check as you complete each task. This will motivate you to keep working as the clock ticks. You can just take a look at family pictures and photos of friends during your break time if you miss them.

Group Tasks

You can group the tasks that you need to finish for the day and ensure that you've done one bunch or cluster before taking a short break. For example, if you have to call several people or complete a Powerpoint presentation, make a pledge to finish each task before giving in to a simple urge. And when you're done with one bundle of tasks and you reward yourself with a disruptive urge, make sure you time yourself so you don't get carried away and you can easily go back to work.

Set a Timer
Making use of a timer to finish tasks and activities, to set a limit for meetings and discussions, and to control your breaks is truly effective. When you know that a timer is set while you're working on a particular task, you get to feel the pressure as the deadline draws nearer. This will push you to work harder and faster.

Block Websites
If social media sites are not blocked in your office, you must learn how to block them yourself in your computer and mobile gadgets so that you won't be tempted to check your notifications or updates. Also take note of the various websites that tempt you to veer away from work.

Remove Physical Temptations
Is it food that distracts you? Perhaps you are easily sidetracked by games on your mobile phone. Or maybe you get distracted by music. Then, as much as possible, you have to get rid of all these factors that distract or tempt you. This way, it will be easier to stay focused.

Plan Mini Celebrations
Celebrating small successes works for many people. Hence, you must plan your own mini rewards or celebrations for accomplishing clusters of work. For example, when you've finished a specific project, then you can promise yourself that you'll finally give in to that ice cream you've been craving. Or when you've completed your quota, you can plan to go window shopping at the mall before going home. This way you have something to

look forward to that will encourage you to keep working despite some interruptions. However, you should try to avoid rewarding yourself with the same temptations or disruptive urges that you're trying to avoid. Also make sure to celebrate when the workday is done already.

If you keep practicing these methods, you'll soon discover how much easier it can be to control your disruptive urges.

IS MUSIC AN INTERRUPTION TO WORK?

For some people, music can be an interruption when they are working. For others, it can actually help them focus better on what they are doing.

When Trying to Absorb New Information
Many studies in the past have tried to explore this concern. Numerous findings show that music can be detrimental when you're trying to memorize or review something. When you're attempting to absorb new information, especially things that are way beyond your knowledge and experience, it can certainly be challenging to do if there's a song playing in the background or if you have headphones on.

On the other hand, some studies indicate that individuals do better on exams when they studied with classical music or their favorite songs on in the background. Perhaps it really depends from person to person.

Thus, it's important that you test it on yourself and find out whether music interrupts or promotes your brain's ability to absorb and recall new information.

When Engaged in Routine and Creative Activities

A lot of people would attest to the fact that music can actually help keep you focused when you're engaged in routine activities such as typing memos or sealing envelopes. After all, such tasks don't really need much brainpower.

The same goes for creative activities. Research shows that people who are painting or doing crafts, those who are editing photos, and even surgeons who are operating actually seem more relaxed and engrossed in their work when listening to good music that they enjoy or that make them feel good.

Relaxing music, though, can work in both ways. At times, when you are too relaxed, you may tend to slack off or feel sleepy. Meanwhile, there are plenty of people who accomplish more when they are less tense and stressed.

When Singing Along with Music

One surefire way that you can become distracted by music is by singing along. Several studies have proven this fact. If you play familiar music or songs that you like to sing along to, there is a greater likelihood that your attention will drift toward the lyrics and rhythm instead of staying focused on the work you're doing.

Few people can multi-task in this way. Oftentimes, the end result is getting much less work finished than if you had not sung along with the music. Therefore, you should choose soothing music with no lyrics. Make sure to avoid overly upbeat or loud music, as well as songs that are too soft or slow.

Indeed, there is no single black or white answer to the question, "Is music an interruption to work?" It depends on the kind of songs as well as on the individual involved. This is why you should get to know yourself in this regard, so that you can use music to your advantage and be able to maximize your time while also producing high quality work.

CHAPTER SIX: MEETINGS

"Meetings get a bad rap, and deservedly so -- most are disorganized and distracted. But they can be a critical tool for getting your team on the same page."

JUSTIN ROSENSTEIN

OVERVIEW

Effective meetings are a crucial part of time management, in that they facilitate communication and delegation in a way that saves time and improves results. Time management can't be implemented by one individual; it takes collaboration and cooperation. You'll benefit immensely from learning how to prepare for and facilitate efficient meetings – and learning to eliminate unnecessary or redundant ones.

3 AMAZING REWARDS OF EFFECTIVE MEETING MANAGEMENT

Many companies and corporate managers tend to overlook the importance of effective meeting management. Most of the time, trainings on time management are given to the leaders of a company but barely touch on how to handle and run meetings efficiently. What they fail to realize is that teaching effective meeting management can be very helpful in improving productivity and reducing the wastage of time.

Boost in Productivity
One amazing reward of excellently managing a meeting is being able to boost your productivity and that of the entire team or department. If you are working on an independent project, you can surely improve productivity by handling meetings well, when you schedule and run them commendably, you will delegate tasks properly and monitor them successfully too. Doing so will encourage people and remind them to deliver on time and perform better. At the same time, meetings will not take up too

much of their time.

Enhancement in Morale

As opposed to a leader who holds meetings but does not facilitate or follow-up effectively, someone who practices superior meeting management is bound to be appreciated and admired. Even more importantly, overall morale will be enhanced, because people will not be demotivated by dragging meetings that they find unproductive and unnecessary.

You should have your team members on your side at all times, understanding why there is a need for some meetings and appreciating how these gatherings are helping in the progress of your tasks and goals. Indeed, when this happens, there is a morale boost which results in better teamwork and results.

Improved Savings

Another reward of effective team management is improved savings. This refers not only to savings of time, but also of effort and money. Instead of using up time that people can utilize for something more productive or important, you can handpick the meetings that ought to push through and those that are not necessary. In this way, you can help your colleagues or subordinates save effort and energy too. These can be directed toward other essential things.

At times, meetings call not only for extra time and effort but also for money because there is a need to travel every now and then, or to spend on food and drinks. Money can also be saved if you opt for a virtual meeting that's paperless and does not necessitate the use of transportation.

These three rewards can make a big difference in a company's overall output. They also contribute to much happier employees who are more likely to stay longer and put greater effort into the company's success. If you understand these benefits, you will realize just how vital it is to ensure effective meeting management within any institution. After all, this is one way of certifying better time management and greater profits for the firm.

5 WAYS TO BOOST YOUR MEETING MANAGEMENT SKILLS

One of the most common time wasters in the office is meetings. No wonder so many employees tend to hate meetings; they find these gatherings redundant and unnecessary. Hence, if you are a supervisor, manager, team leader, or project coordinator, you ought to make sure to work on improving your meeting management skills. This is one great way to ensure that you use your time wisely and avoid wasting others' time as well.

Here are some ways you can boost your meeting management skills:

Define the purpose of the meeting and determine the specific objectives.
You cannot just call a meeting whenever you feel like it. Planning is key in order to have successful meetings without wasting anyone's time. Thus, the first step toward achieving effective assemblies is to define the purpose. What is the meeting for and what do you intend to attain by the end of it? Be sure to state the actual purpose when you send notices to those included. Before the meeting, set the specific objectives without going overboard,

given the time limit.

Prepare the agenda ahead of time and be sure to stick to it.
After defining the purpose and determining the objectives, you must have an agenda prepared before beginning the meeting. Go over it at the start so everybody's on the same page. As you discuss each item, you can tick it off like a regular checklist. Make sure to keep track of the amount of time remaining and prioritize items accordingly with your team as you go along.

Always start on time and do not review topics for those who are late.
It's always prudent to start meetings on time. A common cause of time loss in the office is gathering in a venue and waiting for everyone to be present before starting. This is a huge time waster that should be avoided. It is certainly not fair to those who came early and on time. It's not a healthy practice because people will continue to arrive late, since you wait for them and possibly review topics when they arrive.

Record the minutes of the meeting and send copies to everyone.
It is a big mistake to forego the keeping of meeting minutes. You and others may end up having to guess what was covered and accomplished in prior meetings. Sometimes this results in arguments as well. If you have the minutes written down, recorded, and sent to everyone involved, then you will all be on the same page when it to assigned tasks and deadlines. You will be able to better monitor your progress and avoid repeating the same discussions.

Set a timeframe and keep to it as much as possible.
A meeting should have a concrete timeframe. If it is set for one hour, then make sure you finish within an hour, even if not everything has been covered yet. Unless the topics are very urgent, then you ought to stick to the timeframe. This is one way to show respect for the time of others, regardless of their position or status in the company.

When you practice these five tips, you'll be able to boost your meeting management skills and thus avoid this major time waster. At the same time, your subordinates, team members, and colleagues will surely be grateful, appreciative and more productive.

TECHNOLOGY ADVANCEMENT: HOW IT HELPS IN MEETING MANAGEMENT

Managing meetings is an essential skill that every leader needs. It's highly important not only in the corporate world but in all other fields wherein people have to gather and work together. Since meetings can turn into major time wasters when not managed efficiently, you have to work on improving your own capabilities in this area. The good news is that technological advancement in modern times has paved the way for easier and faster management of meetings.

Use of Scheduling Software
Because of advanced technology these days, a lot of companies and offices are making use of scheduling software. This type of computer program allows people to keep track of the schedules of their colleagues or subordinates in a team or department. For instance, if you already have a meeting set, you can record it into the software so the others will be aware and will not ask you to attend another meeting on the same date and time.

There are several institutions in which most employees have

scheduled tasks and activities, which are recorded using the scheduling software. Hence it is the program that determines the common free time slots of those who have to hold meetings together.

Different Meeting Management Programs
Today there are plenty of meeting management computer programs that can work online or offline. They can be quite helpful in setting meetings among different members of a company or institution and sending reminders days, hours, or minutes before a meeting. Some even include special features such as recording minutes and sending them to those who attended the meeting.

Indeed technology has proven to be very beneficial in meeting management, especially if all employees are regularly connected to their own computers and even hand-held devices.

Employment of Virtual Meetings
With the prominent use of laptops, personal computers, electronic tablets, and smart phones at present, it makes good sense to also employ virtual meetings from time to time. Instead of spending extra time heading over to one venue, several people can just have the meeting over the Internet or via a company's local network. It's also a good way to save money if you are used to having meetings in a restaurant or allotting budget for refreshments.

A virtual meeting refers to two or more people communicating via chat and video conferencing, usually online. Even if you are seated comfortably inside your office or even at home, you can still meet up with your team and discuss your meeting agenda. You don't need to travel, thus saving time and effort that can then be used for other important matters.

Virtual meetings can be held through online programs such as Skype. There are many free and paid websites and software that can facilitate such meetings. Depending on the nature of your business and what you wish to accomplish, you can choose among these various programs to find the one that suits your needs best.

Technological advancement continues to propel meeting management forward. You should definitely jump on the bandwagon if you haven't already. Sooner or later, you'll discover just how beneficial using meeting management software can be for time management and productivity.

TOP 10 REASONS BEHIND WASTEFUL MEETINGS

It has always been said that meetings in the office or in any organization are not an indication of progress. Many individuals in positions of power feel that holding meetings is necessary because it makes them feel more authoritative and in control. It gives them the illusion that their projects are advancing. Nevertheless, these meetings are certainly not a surefire sign of any improvement or success. Most of the time, many subordinates feel that most meetings are just a waste of time.

Here are the top 10 reasons why most meetings translate to wasted time:

Vague Objectives
If you hold a meeting without first identifying your main objectives for having it, it's very likely that you will beat around the bush and not get much done. A lot of time will be used up without accomplishing much. Hence, in the name of effective time management, be sure to identify your objectives and mention them at the beginning of the meeting. As you go along, tick off the corresponding items on your checklist.

Wrong Attendees

It's very important to clearly identify who needs to be in a particular meeting. If you end up with the wrong attendees, you'll just be wasting everyone's time and decreasing productivity.

Too Many People Present
Also avoid including too many people in a meeting because it leads to an increased tendency for most to just ride on and go with the flow without really paying attention or participating the entire time. Just pick the key people and let them hold their own meetings with their subordinates.

Lack of Agenda
Aside from identifying your objectives, you also need to have a clear agenda that you expect or want to be covered for a specific assembly. This way, you are guided accordingly and will not miss out on anything. You also won't end up calling for another meeting.

Inability to Follow Agenda
At times, even if you have a good agenda prepared, there is always a tendency to veer away from the essential matters. Make sure to follow your agenda so that you can avoid wasting time.

Lack of Preparation
When there is lack of preparation, meetings are more likely to drag on without covering important concerns. You might end up discussing plenty of not so urgent and not so important things. Some people may keep contributing anecdotes that take up more time but may not be necessary. Plan ahead to avoid such possibility.

Lack of Results and Action Plans
Be sure to be result-oriented. This means that for every part of your agenda covered, you should also be able to achieve one of your objectives. It also means that the meeting ends with a list of detailed action plans that come with set deadlines.

Late Start
Avoid starting late because this will also mean ending late. Fur-

thermore, people will get irritated when you begin later than the time indicated because every minute may translate to wasted time that they could have used up for something else.

Late Ending

As much as possible, do not end meetings late especially if this means forcing people to stay later than their work hours. They will just get annoyed and will not be able to concentrate anymore. Productivity will go down rather than up when this happens.

Poor Follow-Up

Another common reason behind wasteful meetings is poor follow-up. No matter how efficient a meeting seemed to be, it's bound to go to waste if there is no follow-up on the action plans discussed and set. The meeting will be for nothing if there is no task actually carried out afterward for progress.

CHAPTER SEVEN: PLANNING

"A goal without a plan is just a wish."

ANTOINE DE SAINT-EXUPÉRY

OVERVIEW

A good planner is always conscious of what should be accomplished, on a moment-to-moment basis as well as in the long term. Once you pin down the traits and skills that make for a good planner, you can work to integrate them into your own approach to work and life. Learning to formulate concrete plans and look forward every step of the way will result in heightened productivity and increased achievement of goals.

THE 6 TRAITS OF AN EXCELLENT PLANNER

There's no doubt that planning is an essential part of excellent time management. Sometimes, you encounter individuals in your lifetime who seem to be very good at planning. If you feel as if you still need a lot of improvement in this aspect, it's important for you to note the traits that an excellent planner possesses. This will give you a better idea of how you can become a better planner.

Organized
Naturally, you can't be a good planner if you are not organized. You have to know your vision and goals, be able to identify the actions necessary to achieve them, prioritize well, sort things into various categories, schedule tasks and activities effectively, and come up with a clear system or structure of how to carry out and evaluate your plan.

Detail-Oriented
Superb planning does not only consist of the vision and the big picture. It also entails pinpointing of details included under each goal and each task. When you are detail-oriented, you almost never miss out on anything that has to be done to achieve a goal. You take note of small elements that other people tend to overlook, such as the note that should accompany the tokens for the

special guests or the font size and style that should be used in reports to make it all uniform and professional-looking.

Determined

If you find yourself getting discouraged easily, this is a red flag for you in the planning department! That's because determination is key to effective planning. Oftentimes planners are bound to come across hindrances and setbacks that they must work around or work out to continue moving closer to their goals.

Flexible

Usually, determination goes hand-in-hand with flexibility. Being flexible means you can adjust to any situation especially unexpected ones. You're not the type who suddenly feels lost and dejected when things don't go according to plan. Instead of resigning for the day because of a sudden hitch, you explore the various alternatives available. And so when formulating your plans, you always try to have a Plan B and even a Plan C.

Proactive

Proactive is the opposite of reactive. Let's say the client rejects your work. A reactive person may end up sulking for a long time, spend hours complaining to others, or perhaps even putting down the client. On the other hand, a proactive person will also feel bad but will likely ask how he or she can improve the work and thus spend time working on something better rather than moping around and venting out. This individual makes a better planner because he or she will simply come up with substitute plans when the first one doesn't work out as expected.

Vigilant

When you're vigilant, you are alert and observant. This allows a planner to determine things to watch out for so that the plan can be carried out smoothly toward the realization of a goal. Being on guard is characteristic too of an excellent planner since this will enable closer assessment of tasks and activities as well as viewing of the different angles involved in a plan.

HOW YOU CAN FORMULATE A WORK PLAN AND TIME PLAN

In anything that you want to accomplish, time is of great essence. This means that it's highly important for you to learn how to manage your time effectively before you can actually go further in pursuing your goals.
One of the most crucial aspects of time management is planning. You need to come up with both a work plan and a time plan in order for efficient planning.

The Six Essential Questions
If you're not sure how to go about formulating a work plan and time plan, all you have to do is just ask these six essential questions:

What do I want and expect to accomplish?
Before you start any action or plan any activities, you must have clear goals that give you a vision of your desired results. If these are clear in your mind, then you can plan how to act in order to reach your goals more competently.

What do I need to do so I can accomplish my goals?
Once you've set the goals, the next question to ask is how you get there. Your answer will determine the specific activities that

have to be carried out to achieve your desired outcome.

What do I have to prioritize?
Which one has to come first? Which are the most important and urgent tasks and activities? You need to point out your priorities as well so you don't end up taking too much time with mundane things and then rushing toward the end to finish the more vital matters.

How long will each activity take to complete?
In planning, you must also set the exact time that it will take you to complete each task or activity. This way, you can adjust accordingly to meet deadlines and to have an allowance for emergencies and other sudden concerns.

When should I start and end each activity?
Of course it's also important to make a schedule for all activities. Coming up with a good schedule will do wonders for your plan because it will guide you on what to finish each day and how you can multi-task, adjust, and prioritize.

How flexible can I be when it comes to uncontrollable factors that get in the way?
Don't forget to make room for flexibility because there are always uncontrollable factors that appear along the way. For instance, just when you're scheduled to run your errands, there's suddenly a heavy downpour and you have no choice but to stay at home. In this regard, you ought to allot a few days of adjustment before the actual deadlines.

Take note that the first three questions will help you make a work plan while the last three will assist you in your time plan. Both are extremely and equally important when planning for anything.

Once you have mastered answering the questions given above whenever you plan, you'll find it more of a breeze to realize your goals. What's even better is that you can manage time a lot better and thus avoid unnecessary stress.

THE REAL DEAL ON DAILY PLANS VS. WEEKLY PLANS

Are you the type of person who "lives for the day"? You make a to-do list at the start of each day or perhaps create it the night before a new day. You often find yourself with overlapping tasks or appointments. You sometimes feel lost about which activities to prioritize for the day.

If the above description sounds like you, then you are that "live for the day" person who knows how to plan on a day-to-day basis only.

Is this easy? Yes. Is it ideal? No.

The Pros and Cons of Daily Plans

If you're yearning to effectively manage your time so that you can accomplish more and get to your goals in the shortest time possible, you need to review the pros and cons of daily plans.

Yes, having a daily checklist is surely helpful. You get to have a direction to follow for the entire day. It makes planning easier when you just keep writing down what has to be done for that particular day. What's more, you can even assess your daily success by ticking off what you were able to complete.

But what's the catch?
Daily plans have drawbacks. For one, you can't keep your appointments and activities straight. If a friend invites you to dinner on Saturday, you might say yes without realizing that you've already agreed with your boss to reserve this day for your one-on-one meeting. You have overlooked this because you did not take note of it in your calendar. You did not plan for it because it was many days away when you had that conversation with your boss.

Another drawback--- it's difficult to prioritize. You thought the day was fruitful because you finally met with the suppliers of the company. However, since you did this ahead of meeting with your supervisor, you could not supply some other required info. So now you need to meet with the supervisor and then go back to the suppliers. This waste of time could have easily been avoided if you had a weekly or even a monthly plan.

In addition, using only a daily plan will make you seem blind. You have no foresight so you cannot plan ahead effectively. You will tend to forget things and may spend some days doing tasks that are not necessary.

The Pros and Cons of Weekly Plans
Now what if you make use of a weekly plan instead?

For starters, a weekly plan is great for having a vision to give you direction for the entire week. You can adjust the work and time throughout the days and make room for extras. For example, if you want to have a date with your spouse and children during the weekend, you can do so without slowing down your progress. This is because you can clearly see how you'll divide the needed activities you should do to attain your goals for the week.

Furthermore, it's much easier to foresee and anticipate potential concerns that you can prepare for. Let's say you take a look at your weekly plan and notice that a client presentation is scheduled for Friday. So early on in the week, you already reserved the room and equipment to be used. At times, those who use only a daily plan tend to forget these small details.

Weekly plans also come with a disadvantage. If you had written only "Plan for event" on Tuesday and "Meet with team" on Wednesday, there's a tendency to overlook some elements. Hence you might not be ready to meet yet with the team the next day. Or you might take up more time than usual because it's only during the meeting that those you've forgotten will come up.

It's not enough to see the bigger picture. You also have to zoom in closer to check those little specks. Monitoring of small tasks on a daily basis is necessary to gain success. Prioritizing and preparing for upcoming events and activities throughout the week is also of utmost importance. Therefore, it's vital to make use of both daily plans and weekly plans because each type serves its purpose.

5 COMMON SCHEDULE DISRUPTIONS THAT CAN RUIN YOUR WEEKLY PLAN

When doing your weekly plan, one important consideration you ought to mull over is how much flexibility you're going to put in so as to make sure that you still get to achieve your goal by the end of the week.
Good time management includes flexibility, after all, as there are usually disruptions that occur throughout a regular week which can get in the way of your scheduled tasks and activities.

Below are the 5 common schedule disruptions that can ruin your weekly plan:

Health Concerns
Health matters a great deal when trying to accomplish things within a given period. If you suddenly fall sick, you might not be able to finish the tasks you've assigned to yourself for the day. Of course you can always boost your immune system by eating nu-

tritious food and taking supplements before you even begin the week.

However, there may be times when sickness can't be helped. Besides, what if it happens to someone else on whom you're depending to get something done? In such cases, you should have an allowance of a few days to adjust.

Unexpected Accidents

Perhaps you think it's not likely that your top-performing team member will get into an accident. But that's why it's called an accident. It cannot be foreseen or predetermined.

Accidents may involve not just the people directly working but perhaps those close to them. What if you have a relative in the hospital that you need to take care of?

Accidents can also include other unexpected situations. They can be as simple as spilling juice onto your newly bought suit for an event you're preparing for.

Natural Disasters

Natural disasters like earthquakes, floods, and typhoons cannot be helped. They can happen and cause delay in your work schedule. Thus, it's up to you to make the allowance especially if you've already heard about an impending storm or if you know you're traveling to a place prone to these disturbing weather conditions at a particular season.

Urgent Problems

Urgent problems can range from an irate customer's phone call to a life-and-death situation in the family. They have just one thing in common--- they need to be given attention ASAP. As a result, they cause a disruption in the schedule you carefully laid out for the week. If the schedule is quite tight, then you might end up with plenty of backlogs, missed deadlines, and overlapping tasks later on.

Leisurely Activities

Leisurely activities such as surfing on the Internet, watching TV, and going out with friends should most definitely be avoidable. Thus, you must not let them ruin your weekly plan, or you'll always be going through "crunch time" and dealing with added stress that should have been dodged.

Nonetheless, it's still advisable to make leisure a part of the potential disruptions to your schedule. Even if you've been moving up the self-discipline ladder, there may still be instances when you just can't help giving in. It may be that your best friend is going through a tough time and asks you to have a quick drink. Maybe your busy brother from overseas finally had the time to call you up over the Internet and have a video chat. These moments call for time adjustment.

Knowing these common schedule disruptions will remind you to always be flexible whenever you're doing your weekly plans.

MAKE TIME YOUR SUPERHERO POWER!

CHAPTER EIGHT: PRIORITIES

"Our life is the sum total of all the decisions we make every day, and those decisions are determined by our priorities."

MYLES MUNROE

INTRODUCTION

Learning to prioritize is an essential step along the path to successful time management. Your efficiency will increase dramatically once you begin to organize tasks and activities according to their level of importance and urgency. Prioritizing will help you to identify and complete the most important, difficult, or time-consuming tasks before moving on to subsidiary activities, saving you time, energy and stress in the process. Furthermore, on a broad scale, determining what matters most – and what matters least – is an important act of self-discovery that will aid you in managing all areas of your life, even beyond work.

3 ESSENTIAL CHARACTERISTICS OF PRIORITIES THAT YOU NEED TO LEARN

Sometimes in life, you find yourself at a crossroad. It is in these instances that you realize what your priorities really are. Do you put greater value on family or are you more of the career-driven type? Is money the driving force behind your life or do your relationships matter more? These are just some of the questions you have not pondered on a lot and yet are revealed in your choices and decisions.

In order to provide the proper direction in your life according to your desired future, you need to learn how to prioritize well. However, before you can do this, you have to grasp the essential characteristics of priorities. Having this deeper understanding will enable you to set your priorities straight once and for all.

Priorities are Subjective

Understand that priorities are subjective. There are no wrong or right priorities. They differ from one person to another.

Furthermore, people change. And along with such changes may come priority transformation. What you valued before may not be the same today because of particular influences and experiences over the years.

Knowing that priorities are subjective will help you know your own identity better and develop yourself further in the process, instead of blindly following the priorities of your parents and/or mentors. This realization will also enable you to adjust to your loved ones well even if they do not share the same priorities that you have.

Priorities are Enlightening
Also know that priorities are enlightening.

In what ways? They shed light on what you value. They allow people to glimpse your background, your personality, and your dreams and goals. Of course this doesn't mean you have to hide behind a mask. If your priorities at the moment reflect a not-so-good perception of you in the eyes of others, then allow this to awaken you and to help you rethink your vision for yourself and how you're working toward it.

Priorities are enlightening because they allow even you to know yourself better. Sometimes you think you're this person, but actually you're not. The real you is uncovered through what you prioritize.

Priorities are Influential
Priorities are also influential. They help you set your goals and give direction to your life. Where are you headed? It's all because you chose to prioritize specific things.

These priorities can influence your career, health, relationships, and all other aspects of your life. For example, if you have decided to place greater value on making your business grow but have sacrificed time with your kids, this priority can greatly influence the future. It may mean becoming successful financially and providing all the material things for your children. But what if they end up being rebellious because they are so much in need of attention? What if they have tried to seek love the wrong way?

Now these are consequences that you will need to face, brought about by your priorities in the past.

Of course the situation does not have to be this extreme. You can always choose to balance two, three, or even more areas in your life to be your top priorities. Sometimes it can be truly draining, but if these things matter a lot, you will pull through. You'll get accustomed to juggling these chief priorities which can result in the future you want for yourself.

Indeed realizing these three characteristics of priorities will make you think twice before setting your goals and acting on them. Discover who you really are, what you want in life, and what will make you genuinely happy. This way, you can set your priorities straight, manage your time efficiently, and live a great life.

5 IMPORTANT BENEFITS OF PRIORITIZING

Have you set your priorities straight? Prioritizing your projects and tasks properly plays a gigantic role in time management and essentially in attaining your goals. You have to exert great effort to train yourself in this area and thus improve how you do it.

Here are 5 benefits of prioritizing that contribute to more productive days and to a happier you:

Assignment of Value
When you analyze priorities and sort them accordingly, you are able to assign each one with a particular value. In doing this, you suddenly have a clearer picture of what you ought to be doing first and which one has to take up more time.

Adjustment of Time Allotment
Many people do things randomly and are easily distracted from what they should be working on or spending time on. In prioritizing, not only values are assigned to each task, activity, or project. You also get to designate the amount of time you will spend on each of them in a day, in a week, and also within long-term periods.

Elimination of Distractions

Another great benefit of learning how to prioritize is being able to eliminate distractions. In the various aspects of your life, you will surely encounter a lot of disturbances and diversions that will make you lose your focus. But when you have your priorities set straight, you can easily identify these distractions. It will be simpler to get rid of them or at least limit the time they consume.

Faster Achievement of Goals

When you know how to prioritize well, you get to focus on your goals and work accordingly. You can choose the things that matter more and thus be able to achieve your goals faster. As a result, you can move on to other goals and to bigger dreams that you would like to pursue. Success is bound to follow when you prioritize constantly and consistently.

Creation of Balance

There are many people who are viewed to be successful but are not actually happy. This is probably because they don't have balance in their lives. For instance, numerous individuals may seem financially successful and seem to be going places in their careers. But in their personal lives, they are undergoing domestic problems or perhaps issues within themselves. On the other hand, there are also those who are lucky to have loving families but may not have good relationships outside of their homes. Or they may be experiencing great challenges at work. These situations can be amended through prioritization combined with action. You should certainly prioritize regularly to attain this balance among all areas of your life.

You will certainly gain these 5 important benefits from prioritizing efficiently. Make sure to practice it every single day because priorities can be adjusted on a short-term basis based on what you have accomplished so far.

URGENT VS. IMPORTANT: HOW TO SET YOUR PRIORITIES STRAIGHT

Have you noticed how you always seem to run out of time to do the things you need to accomplish? Do you often find yourself rushing and stressing yourself out just to meet deadlines? Perhaps it's about time you admit to yourself that you are in dire need of help and guidance when it comes to time management.

Setting Your Priorities Straight
Often a lot of people have a problem with setting priorities, which is why they end up wasting numerous hours doing irrelevant things and end up wondering where all the time went at the end of the day.

Do you have your priorities set straight?
Your time management issues may stem from not being able to prioritize well. Yes, there are plenty of different things that you may need to attend to. However, if you know how to balance urgency and importance, then maybe the use of your time can be more effective. Life will be more of a breeze if you can actually

this.

The Four Quadrants of Time Management

Many times, people use up majority of the time attending to pressing problems and deadline-driven undertakings. It leaves them with very little time for their family, hobbies, health concerns, and other things. Another common problem is that when they do not have these very urgent matters to deal with, they tend to relax too much and spend their time doing not-so-urgent and not-so-important things.

Have you heard of the four quadrants of time management presented by the famous author Stephen Covey in his book The 7 Habits of Highly Effective People? This tool evidently exhibits how tasks can be separated distinctly based on urgency and importance. It will guide you in setting your priorities straight.

Quadrant I: Urgent and Important

At times, you find yourself spending 80% to 90% of your time working on urgent concerns such as your deadlines. But if you were able to do these tasks little by little ahead of time, perhaps you will not have to rush them.

Unless there's an emergency or crisis that you immediately have to attend to, you should not be spending a lot of time on tasks that belong in this quadrant.

Quadrant II: Not Urgent But Important

It is said that effective people who are good in time management spend majority of the time doing tasks found in this quadrant. All planning and preparation matters fit in this quadrant. Even relationship-building belongs here. Hence these are things you should be doing to avoid filling up your Quadrant I.

Quadrant III: Urgent But Not Important

Sometimes, you're driven to work on tasks that seem urgent but are actually not important just because you have gotten used to them. It may also be due to requirements at work that you have no control over. In such case, you might want to bring it up in your next meeting so that everyone can be more efficient in the use of time. If there are particular papers and meetings that are unnecessary, maybe you can propose eliminating them or replacing them with better, less time-consuming alternatives.

Usually, the things that fall under this quadrant include minor issues of people around you, needless reports, pointless phone calls and emails, and unnecessary meetings. If you can do without these things, then please avoid them.

Quadrant IV: Not Urgent and Not Important
This quadrant is where all your time-wasters belong to--- browsing on the Internet, excessive TV, too much relaxation activities, chatting about pointless matters, and having a lot of long and unwarranted breaks.

There is a huge temptation to dwell in this quadrant, which will definitely make you end up with almost no time anymore to do the important tasks. Be sure to catch yourself before falling into this rut.

Once you truly understand these four quadrants and have mastered them, you need to practice doing only the important things, whether urgent or not. Keep practicing until it becomes a habit. Of course you still deserve to relax and have fun, but limit these activities and you'll do just fine.

5 TIPS TO HELP YOU PRIORITIZE BETTER

Is prioritization a major weakness of yours? Is it your "kryptonite"?

Don't fret. You don't have to live with it, because you can actually work on improving your time management skills.

The time on your hands doesn't have to always keep running out each day. You don't need to panic as if you're always listening to a ticking bomb. It's all a matter of prioritizing.

Here are 5 important tips you can apply to help you prioritize better and ultimately manage your time well too:

Determine what's important.
Sometimes you believe that you are fully aware of the important tasks and things in your life that you ought to focus on. Nevertheless, you sometimes mistake urgent concerns for what's important. The first lesson you ought to learn in prioritizing is to be able to distinguish between what's urgent and what's important. Once you have this settled, the next lesson is to stick mostly to what you deem important.

Naturally, there will always be situations that call for you to deal with urgent matters. However, if you spend a lot of time planning and preparing the essentials, you can surely lessen the likelihood of urgent things.

Don't get swayed by trivial things.
No matter how good you are in telling important and urgent apart, if you always get swayed by trivial matters, you will still not achieve good time management.

Let's say you start the day with a checklist of things to do, which consist only of those that are important. In the middle of the day, your friend calls you up to discuss her wedding plans. You get caught up in the excitement and start browsing through the Internet for décor ideas to suggest to your friend. Before you know it, two hours of your time had been eaten up!

Sounds familiar? This is an example of getting swayed by trivial things which you can essentially put aside first.

Learn to say no to people.
Oftentimes, another common problem that serves as a hindrance in effective time management is the requests of other people which get in the way of your tasks. Although it's always great to do small (and sometimes big) favors for your family and friends, you should also know how to say no. At the very least, you can also negotiate instead of putting this task above your own priorities.

It's vital to learn the art of saying no. Depending on the person you're talking to, there are various ways to reject the request in a tactful and reasonable manner. Or you may want to negotiate the deadline and the amount of work involved.

Stop switching priorities frequently.
Are you the type of person who often shifts from one priority to another? If this is the case, your focus will certainly be disrupted. You'll never get to the finish line if you keep changing your mind and thus also switching tasks.

At the very beginning, you have to set your priorities straight so you won't need to switch them later on unless the situation really, really calls for it.

Avoid placing yourself in tempting situations.

Lastly, you ought to avoid placing yourself in situations that will tempt you. For instance, if your priority is to graduate with honors, then you know that you're supposed to be studying hard for your upcoming exam.

Now what if your cousin suddenly invites you to his birthday bash? It's just going to be quick. You can just drop by and hang out for a while. Hhmmm… you know that's not going to happen. When you're there already, you will likely end up going back home late. Hence, the logical thing to do here is to avoid going so you will not be tempted.

Try following these 5 tips and you'll definitely be able to prioritize better and thus improve the way you manage your time.

THE PARETO PRINCIPLE: HOW IT CAN HELP YOU IMPROVE TIME MANAGEMENT

Have you ever heard of the so-called 80-20 rule or what is officially recognized as the Pareto Principle? Vilfredo Pareto was an Italian economist originally came up with this formula to describe how only 20% of people in his country actually owned 80% of the overall wealth. Soon it became known as the Pareto Principle, with many individuals in various sectors of society and industries applying the same notion in their areas.

What the Pareto Principle Means Today
Today, the Pareto Principle is widely used in different industries but most especially when it comes to management. It basically refers to the observed fact that only 20% of all you work on will truly make an impact, while 80% is just trivial. In the same way, it also appears true that 20% of problems in an organization are worth paying attention to because this is the percentage that can

create a stir. The 80% is mostly not worth your time.

How It Can Help You Improve Time Management
Remember that what you focus on grows.

The bigger tendency of most people is to focus on many different things that do not really matter. Sure you make them grow but you don't really get any significant benefit in the end. What you ought to do is to pinpoint the 20% that really counts. Focus on this smaller percentage and you will be astonished by the results.

Think of the multitude of tasks that you are faced with every day. Which of these make up the important 20%? Try to list down just the activities that are related to your work. Now from this list, check those that you believe will help you achieve your end goals faster and with greater quality. Even if you do all the things in the list, you should exert more effort in accomplishing those you've checked. After all, these are the ones that can bring about your desired outcome.

Working Smart
Are you working smart or just working hard?

If you don't seem to be going further as you wish no matter how much time you're devoting to work, perhaps you are only working hard. It may be that you are not able to prioritize what ought to be put first. This is why even after many days, weeks, and months of exhaustion, you're still stuck in the same place where you started.

Avoid tiring yourself unnecessarily. Choose to work smart by simply determining the crucial 20% that you have to focus on. Do you really need to keep meeting your team or perhaps you can lessen the meetings and spend more time overseeing the tasks and improving your relationship with your people? Do you really have to use up many hours on filing documents when you can delegate this task to someone and instead start planning the actual project?

Ensure that the tasks included in the 20% are accomplished well and not haphazardly so that you can work smart on the right things and move closer to realizing your goals.

Once you have internalized the Pareto Principle and learned how to truly work smart on the 20%, you will certainly be able to manage your time wisely. Apply it not only in your work, but even in other aspects of your life.

MAKE TIME YOUR SUPERHERO POWER!

CHAPTER NINE: PROCRASTINATION

"Procrastination is like a credit card: it's a lot of fun until you get the bill."

CHRISTOPHER PARKER

INTRODUCTION

P rocrastination is a bad habit that even the most talented and intelligent individuals suffer from. Putting difficult or involved tasks off until a later time will not only cause you to miss the occasional deadline. It will also negatively impact the overall quality of your work, as you rush to produce results at the last possible moment. Many believe that stress causes individuals to procrastinate, but this is only half of the truth; it is important to remember that procrastination in turn causes undue and overwhelming amounts of stress that could be minimized if the tasks in question were completed earlier. Read on for tips and techniques to help you address this common time-waster.

PROCRASTINATION: AN ENEMY OF TIME MANAGEMENT

Are you the type of person who always seems to put off difficult tasks in your list for later? Do you often notice yourself getting preoccupied with things which are not that important instead of plunging head-on into the more challenging jobs you need to accomplish? Then you're trapped inside the procrastination dilemma too--- a maze where you can easily get lost and be misled to believe that you are actually getting things done and moving forward.

Your Worst Enemy is Yourself
When it comes to time management, the worst enemy you can ever have is yourself. And procrastination is known to be one of the most difficult habits that people tend to practice in a vicious cycle which they can't manage to shake off.

If you want to manage your time more wisely and thus progress better in the different aspects of your life, you should drop your do-it-later attitude right this moment. Take a good look at your checklist for the week or for the day and begin with the most unpleasant and those that appear to be the most problematic and demanding. If you don't, you'll cause more problems in the future. These will get dragged further and bring about other glitches and even setbacks to your goals.

It's time to stop focusing on why others are causing delay in your work and how various factors in the environment are hindering you from advancing. Usually, you really cannot control these things so it's much better to just focus on what you can control--- yourself.

Change Your Procrastination Habits

One important step that you can take right now and will surely make a big difference in your success is to change your procrastination habits. Take on a do-it-now approach and stop justifying or defending the habits that you've gotten used to in the past.

If you have to call up that hard-to-deal-with person, do so now so you can set it aside or act on it further in order to go forward. If you have been ignoring the huge pile of papers on your table for quite some time now, it's high time for you to face the music and heave a big sigh of relief when you've finally cleared them up and marked them done.

It's essential for you to admit first that you are actually procrastinating. Try to observe yourself from another person's point of view and discover what you have to change. Also take note of the negative effects that your procrastination habits have been causing. Afterward, think of the amazing benefits that you can enjoy once you have overcome the tendency to procrastinate.

Indeed you must realize that setting aside something for later or even completely ignoring it will not make it vanish into thin air. Rather, you are just making the task bigger by delaying it. You're also causing yourself more stress in the process.

Starting today, make it a habit to tick off first from your checklist the things that are unpleasant and that involve tough decisions. Sooner or later, you'll be happy to see that this simple change will lead you faster to success.

CONQUERING PROCRASTINATION: HOW TO PLAN AND IMPLEMENT ACTION

In every goal that you wish to accomplish, it is always crucial to have a plan first before implementing any action. This way, you can clearly visualize what you desire and how you can benefit from it before you lay down the cards for pursuing this particular vision or goal.

Planning
To conquer procrastination effectively, you need to plan your actions. Here are the things you should include in your plan:

Old Habit to Eliminate
You have to be clear about the old habit/s that you would like to get rid of. Be specific. Instead of just writing "I want to stop procrastinating", you ought to write "I want to change my habit of avoiding the writing of memos and making of reports".

New Habit to Develop
It's not sufficient to just list the old habit you with to eliminate or change. You need to also clarify the new habit you would like

to develop. Following the example given above, you can write in this section something like "Starting today, I will do first the tasks involving written work in the office".

Steps for a Strong Start

When you have specified the new habit you want to develop, you should then write down the steps that you can take in order to start strong. For instance, you can ask a superior or colleague to train and guide you on writing memos and making reports in the office. Another step could be to work on this sort of tasks early and little by little every day.

Steps to Avoid Straying from Your New Habit

What steps can you take to help prevent you from straying? Perhaps you can ask your boss to be stricter with deadlines and to give you small reminders regularly. You may also set an alarm in your PC or laptop to always prompt you to keep working on your new habit. Furthermore, you can decide on a small prize for yourself such as a spa treat at the end of the week if you don't stray from your new habit. Choose a picture that will remind you of this treat and turn it into your computer's wallpaper.

People to Help You Conquer Procrastination

It's vital to have others to help you out as you make your way toward establishing and maintaining your new habit while getting completely rid of the old. List the people who can help you and the specific ways you believe they can do to be of great assistance.

Implementing

Now that your plan is all set, of course you should quickly move to the implementation part. This can also be a difficult stage as you have to stick to your plan and be successful in conquering procrastination. Hence you must also determine methods on monitoring yourself and moving forward in small steps.

Find someone whom you can share your plans with and be accountable to. You can come up with a written contract with both of your signatures. Include here a nice reward you can look forward to so that you'll have something to hold you back from straying or giving up.

It's also important to note why you want to do this. What will you get after you have conquered procrastination? Fill your surroundings and things with reminders about the benefits you desire.

Keep a calendar that contains deadlines for the actions you have planned. Mark each day that you are able to keep to the new habit and give yourself the challenge to do it for at least 30 days straight.

Conquering procrastination is certainly a big challenge in itself. But once you nail it, you are bound to enjoy a tremendous sense of freedom and find yourself getting more done and getting them done faster.

THE 5-STEP PLAN TO BATTLING PROCRASTINATION

Perhaps your procrastination tendencies have been eating up your time and energy, therefore hindering you from achieving your objectives and meeting deadlines. Yes, a lot of people often procrastinate. It's a normal tendency for many to put off the hardest things they have to deal with. It's always easier to go with what's uncomplicated. Nevertheless, simple daily acts of procrastination can get the better of you and can push you downhill without your being aware of it.

Here's a 5-step plan that you can apply in order to battle procrastination:

Step 1 - Acceptance

The first step is for you to accept the fact that you are actually procrastinating. If you keep rationalizing or justifying your actions, then you will not be motivated to fight the propensity for it. You'll just keep doing it and will get stuck in these bad habits that can greatly affect success in various aspects of your life.

Step 2 - Analysis

Once you have accepted the truth about your procrastination habits, you should analyze them. Study yourself and write down the things you often put off for later. Take note of the reasons why you always seem to delay doing these things.

Step 3 - Action

Understanding your own procrastination habits will enable you to take the right action. If you find that you always postpone things that involve talking to people because you're not confident enough or you don't have good communication skills, then at least you know what to work on. But don't wait until you've improved in this area before tackling such activities. No matter how challenging it may seem, just do it and get it over and done with. You'll discover yourself feeling a lot better and having more time on your hands for the rest of the day.

Step 4 - Alleviation

It is totally plausible that numerous individuals procrastinate to avoid the unpleasant and the difficult. What you can do is to alleviate the burden by delegating certain tasks to other people who may be more capable or may actually enjoy the things you don't want to do. You may also opt to break down some tasks into little stages so you can take them on one step at a time. This way, you can avoid becoming overwhelmed by all the negative feelings.

Step 5 - Appreciation

As you complete one small task under the bigger challenge you're facing, take the time to congratulate yourself and appreciate what you have accomplished. These little successes are very important. Soon you'll find yourself getting used to undertaking the toughest tasks first.

Always remember to pat yourself on the back every time you take on a huge task or a tough job. Show appreciation to yourself through a mini reward, silent praise, or simple celebration. This way, you always feel good right after tackling one of these things that you usually stay away from.

When you follow these 5 steps, you're bound to win the battle against procrastination and be well on your way to success and abundance.

THE 6 DON'TS OF THE FIGHT AGAINST PROCRASTINATION

Are you ready to fight against your very own procrastination tendencies, the habits that you have been practicing for many years now? Have you finally admitted to yourself that you are actually procrastinating and that it has been getting in the way of your victory? Well then, you ought to be fully aware of what you should NOT do when it comes to the combat against procrastination.

Don't Rationalize
The very first don't--- Do NOT rationalize.

"I can't start this task because I don't have enough time to finish it today."

"I can't play with my children because I have plenty of work to do and this is important for me to get that promotion which is also for them, anyway."

"I can't talk to my boss now because the report is not yet complete and I'm still waiting for the client's final decision."

The sample statements above are just some of the ways you seem to rationalize your putting off of a task. Deep inside yourself, you very well know that the task should be done now and that it can actually be done despite your conditions and reasons. Remember that if you keep rationalizing, you will never get anywhere. You will never be able to change your procrastination habits.

Don't Wallow in Self-Pity

Do you have that inclination to wallow in self-pity because you were not able to finish your checklist for the day? Do you feel sorry for yourself every time something doesn't go your way during the day, hence causing you to become paralyzed and not be able to accomplish anything?

If your answer is 'yes' to these questions, you're bound to procrastinate often just because you feel down. And when you put off things and end up with more items on your list the next day, you again feel sorry for yourself and thus immerse yourself in self-pity rather than be productive. It's a rancorous cycle that's difficult to get out from if you don't exert enough effort to stop self-pitying right now.

Don't Depend on Your Mood

Many people do some tasks when they are "in the mood". What if you never get into that mood to do a certain activity? What if inspiration doesn't strike and you're already way past the deadline? Other things will just pile up on top of what you haven't done and these will cause even greater problems.

It's imperative that you do not depend on your mood to get things done. There is no right mood. Once you get started, the task will seem to ease up along the way.

Don't Be a Perfectionist

There are just some things that involve risks. Actually, most things are risky. Hence, you cannot play it safe and hesitate to complete a task just because you're afraid of not getting it right or of running into a huge boulder.

Keep in mind that it's okay not to get perfect results. Just do your best and learn from your mistakes.

Don't Give In to Temptation
Even if you have already begun fighting procrastination, there is always that temptation to go back to your old habits. After all, it's much easier to put off things and act according to what you have gotten used to.

No matter how uncomfortable it gets, just keep going and never give in to temptation. Or else, you might find yourself back at square one.

Don't Ever Stop
In the fight against procrastination, it's not enough to get started. You have to keep moving forward. It's important NOT to stop even if things seem more challenging and unpleasant. Keep your eyes on the prize so that you don't lose the focus. Remember that you are doing this to improve your time management and essentially your entire life.

MAKE TIME YOUR SUPERHERO POWER!

CHAPTER TEN: SCHEDULING

"The key is not to prioritize what's on your schedule, but to schedule your priorities."

STEPHEN COVEY

OVERVIEW

Scheduling is one of the most concrete and easily implemented strategies that can help you to develop superior time management skills. Allotting time for every activity – from professional tasks to chores at home to leisure time with family and friends – will help you to account for every hour of every day, and make the most of each and every one. Once you begin to block out your time into a practical schedule, you will find that you complete tasks faster, more thoroughly, with better results – and less stress.

PLANNING VS. SCHEDULING: WHAT'S THE DIFFERENCE?

A lot of people make the mistake of interchanging planning and scheduling. The result: they tend to just decide on what to do without incorporating the actual timetable for all of these tasks and activities. This is a huge blunder that can lead you to waste time on unnecessary things, to miscalculate the time you have left to accomplish something, and to become stressed over piled up pending jobs.

Lists vs. Blocks
Take a look at your plans. Whether these are the tasks you intend to complete for the week or just for the day, these usually consist of to-do lists that you can easily tick off as you finish each. The problem here, however, is that you won't be able to effectively balance the time you have or make good use of it if there are no specific schedules included.

Planning is all about making lists while scheduling is more of using blocks. When you try to imagine a calendar for organizing your plans, what you picture is blocks of time for an entire month. Sometimes weekly organizers are used too, showing one block for each day. Days are further broken down into blocks of hours.

For efficient time management, you ought to spread out the items in your list in these blocks. This way, you get to clearly see too which items are targeted for the month or if they are to be completed within the day only or even within just one hour!

Intention vs. Commitment
You have to take note that planning only deals with your intention to do things. But then, planning by itself may go to waste if not coupled with scheduling. It will not drive you to accomplish the items in your list because there are no pressuring deadlines included. Hence, this is where scheduling comes in. It enables you to commit.

Planning and scheduling should go hand in hand, just like your intention and commitment to get things done. This way, you're able to manage your time more wisely. You can avoid missing out on items, dropping them, or running out of time to do them.

Knowing the Difference
Now that it's a lot clearer to you how planning and scheduling differ and how they ought to work together, you should be able to efficiently prepare for and manage your projects not only at work but at home. When you plan and schedule, you should definitely include all aspects of your life--- the tasks in the office, cooking dinner, helping the kids with homework, doing the laundry, meeting your best friend for coffee, going to church, etc.

Knowing the difference between planning and scheduling and applying this knowledge will surely help you handle life as a whole in a better way. It might be difficult at first, but with practice, you're sure to improve over time. You'll find yourself relaxing more, feeling more in control, and achieving more of your goals.

4 ESSENTIAL TIPS TO HELP YOU HAVE AN EFFICIENT SCHEDULE

Does it always seem as if you're running after time? If so, this only means that you don't have an efficient schedule which is crucial in time management. Without properly managing your time, you're bound to always go off-course in trying to pursue and fulfill your goals in life.

Here are 4 essential tips that you can follow in order to make your schedule more efficient:

Review Your Supposed Free Time.

Despite the fact that you've been keeping an updated schedule and organizing your tasks and activities regularly, why is it that you seem to have no free time? Look closely into the blocks of time that you have set as your supposed free periods. Are they really considered free time which you can use for leisurely activities of your choice? Or are these hours set for chores and errands that you just cannot put aside such as doing the laundry and going to the grocery?

It's very important to make sure that you have several hours each week allotted only for recreation and relaxation items on your list. After all, you can't always keep your schedule packed or else everything might end up falling apart. Remember that you're human and you can only do so much.

Analyze Your Time-Consuming Errands

There are plenty of time-consuming errands that are not necessarily urgent or important. Hence, you ought to analyze which ones you really need to prioritize for the week or for the day. You should also take note of those that you can actually delegate to others while you focus on more important tasks. What's more, another way you can improve your schedule and handle your time better is to combine some activities based on physical proximity and on significance.

Take Out Time and Energy-Draining Activities

Aside from your time-consuming errands, there may also be other activities that will take a toll on your time and energy without any real benefit. For instance, there are people who can spend hours and hours playing computer games even when they are at work. There are also those who unceasingly complain about their work, bash their superiors, and gossip about colleagues. These situations don't really hold any real value and may not contribute anything positive to your life. Thus, you should make a huge effort to avoid these and take them out of your daily routine or weekly schedule.

Be Proactive When Scheduling

In time management, it's also very important to be proactive. This means that you need to anticipate the difficulties you may encounter in the future and come up with advanced plans to better handle these things or to avoid them from happening or worsening. When you do this, you'll surely be able to prevent problems that often take up enormous chunks of time that you could have used for other productive matters.

Indeed following these 4 simple but essential tips can do wonders for your schedule and thus also promote much healthier and more efficient time management.

THE GREAT BENEFITS OF SETTING APPOINTMENTS

Y ou've always heard of the great importance of appointment setting, but never really got to incorporating this habit into your system. Now you find yourself always running to catch up with deadlines, always wondering where the hours went to. This is why you need to take it seriously this time. Learn how to set appointments... even with yourself.

What you can do is to assign weekly appointment slots, different ones for various things. For instance, you can set aside your Wednesday morning and Thursday afternoons for meetings with your team or with your boss. Of course you have to work this out too with the other people involved before deciding on the slots.

You should also assign one or more slots for appointments that are not regularly done, such as with a customer who has a special request. At least you can also offer these schedules in case there are people who wish to discuss something work-related with you.

It's also essential to assign appointment slots for quality time with loved ones. For example, you can allot your Sunday afternoons for the family.

Lastly, make sure to also have appointment slots for yourself. These are the blocks of time which you can use for your "me" time.

What are the great benefits that appointment setting can bring about? Below are the specific benefits you're bound to enjoy:

Reduced Disruptions
When you set appointments for different things that you have to attend to for the week, you can definitely lessen your disruptions. This way, you know which you must focus on for a certain period or schedule.

For instance, instead of checking emails at different times each day or whenever you feel like it, you can schedule this task every morning or after you're done with all your work at the end of each day. Then you won't have to be bothered by it while working on something else.

Efficient Monitoring
When there are specific times for particular things, it also becomes easier and faster to monitor your progress or what you had accomplished the previous week. It's much simpler to look at all the Tuesday afternoons in your calendar, for instance, if you want to check whom you have talked to so far in your team and what you have covered.

Respect for Others' Time
When you know how to set appointments, this is also one way that you can show respect for the time of other people. It is certainly more professional and will also give them a chance to schedule the other items on their list more effectively.

Less Stress
Because you have allotted appointments for everything you need to do, even going to the grocery or going out with your spouse on a date, you'll soon find yourself having more free time and not feeling as if you're going crazy because of too much

stress. This way, too, you can avoid getting burned out.

More Accomplishments
Knowing how to set appointments is an important part of scheduling your tasks and activities. Consequently, this will significantly contribute to your getting more done. More accomplishments will then lead you to succeed in reaching your goals.

3 IMPORTANT WAYS YOU CAN GET AN EARLY START

Whether you want to face it or not, getting an early start is always better if you wish to accomplish more. Time management becomes more of a breeze when you're able to begin ahead of time.

What exactly does it mean to get an early start?

Being an Early Bird
As the saying goes, "An early bird catches the worm." Whatever you need to have done for the day, starting early in the morning will definitely help you achieve your goal and get ahead of the pack. Some individuals would also say that this is ideal because it puts you in work mode early too, which can define your mood for the rest of the day. As a result, you'll find yourself more successful in following your plans and schedule.

However, an early start in this particular manner does not work for people who are nocturnal in nature. They always seem to feel sleepy and act slow in the morning, so they tend to slack off or choose to do easier and unimportant tasks. If this sounds like you, then better try one of the other ways below.

Getting to Work at Once

The second important way that you can have your early start is by getting to work at once as soon as you settle in your workplace. Instead of chatting with colleagues, reading the newspaper, or drinking coffee as you check your Facebook account, you can immediately get started on the activities you have planned and scheduled for the day.

This is more challenging, though, for home-based and freelance work. In such case, you really have to set a specific time of starting work. When you commit to begin at 9:00 in the morning, turn this into a habit and don't waste time doing other things before you finally start your actual work.

Kicking Off Projects Ahead of Time
Starting early can also mean commencing planned projects ahead of schedule. If you find yourself with some free time in between projects, you can choose to immediately jump to the next one. This will give you greater lead time in the process and will thus provide allowance when meeting deadlines.

In case you were not able to allot enough time for possible interruptions and delays for the duration of the project, then getting a head start will certainly help a lot.

Of course you should also give yourself a break and a reward especially in between big projects. This doesn't mean you can't still get a head start on the next one. You just have to limit your break.

In doing any of these 3 things and especially in doing all of them, you'll find yourself becoming more productive and having much less crunch time. You'll discover just how much stress you're removing from your life by simply doing this. Furthermore, you will learn how to schedule more capably in the future which in turn will boost your time management skills.

HOW TO EFFECTIVELY SCHEDULE YOUR QUIET TIME

Oftentimes, even when you plan and schedule your tasks and activities well, you still end up with a lot of undone items in your list. And majority of the time, this is brought on by your failure to schedule for quiet time.

What is Quiet Time?
Admit it. No matter how much you try to ignore distractions while working, there are usually a lot of small, unimportant matters that tend to drive your attention away from what you're trying to focus on. Think email and social media notifications, phone calls and text messages, colleagues coming up to talk, and other interruptions. Of course there are really times when you need to attend to these things immediately. However, they're just interruptions most of the time.

One way to make sure that such things don't get in your way is to schedule your quiet time--- a blocked period of time each day wherein you can concentrate on your work without being bothered. This means not only choosing a good venue, but also turning off your phone and notifications and staying away from other potential distractions.

How Can You Schedule Your Quiet Time Effectively?

Choose a time of the day that disruptions don't come often. Sometimes there are "dead" hours in the office or at home which you can instead dedicate to working on important tasks. These hours vary, depending on your workplace and the nature of your industry. If you work at home, it will also depend on the schedule of people living with you.

Allot a time for answering calls, updating your social media accounts, and the like so that you don't feel the urge to leave what you're doing just to turn to these things. Slowly but surely, you can make it a habit just like eating lunch at 12 noon. This way too, you can inform people too to contact you only at a particular time of the day.

Choose a great venue where you can really stick to your quiet time without any problem. This can be a library, an empty conference room, or a study. Make sure that the place is devoid of anything that you know will easily divert your attention. It should also be a place that is conducive for working on what you need to accomplish. For example, if you choose your bedroom, this may be a quiet area but it might tempt you to sleep or rest instead. If you select your garden, it can be relaxing on one hand but may give you a view that makes you want to engage in other things.

Of course, you also have to discipline yourself. Quiet time will not work if you cannot control your urges or overcome the temptations. Why don't you try it for just an hour or two first and then hike it up as you go along? You can also assign longer quiet time only if it's crunch time in the office or if you have a big project coming up.

Quiet time can be highly valuable in helping you improve your time management when you get to implement it seriously and continuously.

CHAPTER ELEVEN: TEAM TIME

"Teamwork is the ability to work together toward a common vision. The ability to direct individual accomplishments toward organizational objectives. It is the fuel that allows common people to attain uncommon results."

ANDREW CARNEGIE

OVERVIEW

Exceptional time management cannot be attained by a lone individual. Imagine: you've perfected planning, goal-setting, scheduling and all of the other crucial components of time management. However, if you've failed to share these new techniques and strategies with your team, you are, in many ways, right back at square one. Applying time management skills in the context of your professional team takes coordination and cooperation, but it's well worth your while; once you master team time management, you will find that you work more effectively together, with mutual respect and superior results.

WHAT IS ACCOUNTABILITY AND WHY IS IT IMPORTANT IN TEAM TIME MANAGEMENT?

Just as a mom is accountable for her children, you as a team leader are also accountable for the actions and results of your team members.

Let's say a huge and very important company event was assigned to your department. When it turns out to be a flop because your team members did not coordinate well and ended up rushing a lot of things during the last minute, do you think you can step back and take the blame away from yourself? Of course not.

You're the leader. You're always accountable to and for the team.

Accountability Defined

Accountability is often described as being liable for something or someone. It also refers to answerability or blameworthiness.

More often than not, when accountability is present, there is greater success in any endeavor. It is because people generally tend to exert greater effort when they need to answer to somebody else or are held responsible for something.

This is specifically why you must strive to build a strong sense of accountability within your team and not just between you and the team as a whole. Each person in the team should feel accountable to and for every one of the members as well as you.

The Role of Accountability in Team Time Management
Managing time wisely in a team is naturally important. It's a crucial part of getting things done on time, accomplishing more in a given period, and being successful as a whole.

Just imagine if you're part of a team and you're liable for no one but yourself. There's a greater temptation to slack off, to not do your best because you will not be blamed for anything anyway. You're not going to be held responsible for the mediocre job you did.

On the other hand, you're likely to work harder and faster if you are accountable to and for your teammates. This is because at the back of your mind, you don't want to fail all of these people especially if you care about them. You also don't want to have to answer to the team leader for the errors you committed. It's a position everyone normally wants to avoid.

In this regard, accountability can really do wonders for team time management because each member is more driven to perform well and to deliver on time.

How to Develop Accountability in a Team
If you are currently leading a team, make sure to include the improvement of accountability in your immediate goals. It can truly benefit you and the team in the long run.

From the very beginning, develop a culture of accountability in your team. Have team-building sessions every now and then wherein you break up the team into pairs and groups. The games and activities should aim to build this culture of accountability. Offer team incentives as well as give team punishments.

Assigning buddies or triads will also help. Even if they are placed in different committees, for example, they should still look out for one another to ensure that tasks are carried out punctually and proficiently.

During meetings, you need to call everyone's attention to both successes and aspects that may need improvement. Don't single anyone out in order to avoid outright shaming. You should still do this in a respectful manner that will not offend anyone. Ask each person to contribute ideas on how to improve. At the same time, involve everyone in the celebration of even small successes.

Always remember to be a good example. Openly remind the team that you are accountable to and for them and make sure to show this through your actions, such as in seeking their growth and defending them when necessary. This can also be exhibited through your dedication and perseverance to always have spectacular outcomes in all undertakings.

Once you've established a culture of accountability in the team, you're one step closer to much better team time management.

6 EFFECTIVE WAYS TO IMPROVE TEAM TIME MANAGEMENT

Being a good time manager is one thing. Practicing good time management in a team is another. It certainly takes a different set of skills to become successful in handling time as a group.

Team time management is all about working together to achieve a common goal within a given schedule that all members have agreed upon. It involves setting of objectives, distribution of tasks, and collaboration of efforts in which each aspect and even the smallest undertaking may affect the entire project, the results of particular facets, and/or the other members of the group.

Indeed, mastering team time management is much more challenging than getting to grips with individual time management. Nevertheless, it is a vital proficiency in any organization, no matter what the size of your team is.

Of course, there are various ways in which you can improve your team time management. Whether you're the leader of the group, an assistant to the leader, or simply a member, proposing these simple methods for the enhancement of the team's collective ability to manage time will undoubtedly do wonders for all the future ventures that you will engage in.

Here are 6 effective ways, tested and proven in different settings, that you can implement in your own team to improve team time management:

Respect
Respecting everyone on the team is of great essence. It's not just about listening to their ideas, but showing respect for their time and efforts by being punctual during your meetings and by making sure you complete your part in the project. You have to keep in mind that if you fail to finish your assigned task, it may affect someone else's performance. If you slack off, it may disrupt the entire schedule that the team is trying to follow to meet the set goals.

Plan
You need to plan how you'll carry out a particular project. Who will do which job? Who has to attend which meeting? Who has to talk to which person? There are many things to be accomplished, and thus planning will surely help all the team members divide the allotted time to complete individual and group tasks.

Coordinate
Any group undertaking will not be successful if the members do not coordinate with each other. Learn to discuss and update team members as you finish small tasks. Also ask and never assume if you're not certain.

Deliver
As much as possible, you have to ensure on-time delivery of your own assignments. In this manner, you are subtly showing people how you value them and their time and efforts. It's a great way of earning their respect and encouraging them to do the same.

Save
One important way you can improve team time management is

by continuously making attempts to save time not just for yourself, but for others and for the entire group. For instance, if you have completed your portion of the project, you can volunteer to help others. As a team, you may also categorize some tasks according to proximity and convenience in order to save more time in the process.

Nurture

Did you know that nurturing your relationship with the people you work with can do spectacular things for your team and for the project at hand? When you take the time to hang out with team members for fun, to laugh with them and get to know them more, and to show that you care, the team dynamics significantly progress. When this happens, friendship develops and trust and respect deepen. Hence, you'll discover that you and the others are more willing to sacrifice and exert a bigger effort because you want to and not because you need to.

Practice these methods of improving team time management and you'll find your team getting to achieve more, becoming closer, and soaring to greater heights.

UTILIZING A TEAM TIME LOG TO IMPROVE TEAM TIME MANAGEMENT

Is your team always behind on schedule? Do the members of your team seem to easily brush off deadlines and meetings? Then perhaps it's about time that you plan and implement a time management program for the entire team, one that would emphasize the essential values of respect and communication.

The Advantages of Using a Team Time Log

An important tool that you need to introduce to your team is the team time log. It's definitely a must-have in your program because of the great advantages that it can bring to the table.

Utilizing the team time log will get everyone into the habit of monitoring the whole group's progress when it comes to managing time as well as checking the particular areas where help and guidance are needed.

Moreover, this log is a remarkable way of directing the team toward creating a culture of accountability. Once this kind of culture has been established, it will be much easier for the team members to have a greater sense of responsibility concerning their colleagues. Hence, one would begin to think twice before slacking off on finishing a task. One would also feel troubled and anxious when running late for the group meeting. The end result is people exerting much more effort to do what is expected of them.

How to Make and Use a Team Time Log
You can certainly create your own team time log which can focus on the specific needs of your group. Just remember to keep it simple and straightforward so that people will not get turned off answering it and so that it will only take you a short while to complete it.

In coming up with the log, it's better to encourage the participation and contribution of everyone in the team. This way, they will also have that sense of ownership and will thus be more willing to partake in making it work. Ask their opinions about which exact aspects of time management should be prioritized. From here, together you can formulate the questions for the team time log.

Limit the questions to just three in a sheet, which the team can answer together on various occasions to check if there are improvements. Make the questions open-ended, such as "What can I do to help increase team productivity?" and "Which factors hold us back from meeting deadlines and how can we address and correct these?" It's up to you how you would like the members to answer. You can divide everyone into pairs or smaller teams if you're a big group. If not, each person can contribute an answer to every question posed. Then the floor is open for further discussion after everyone has said their piece.

Once you believe that the objectives for these questions have been met, then that's the time you can move on to other questions that can further improve team time management.

Remember to praise even the smallest improvements and

achievements of the team when it comes to attaining your time management goals. Celebrate small successes in order to deepen the bonding of the group. This way, you can also nurture the relationship among the members and further enhance the values of respect and communication in the process. When this happens, sooner or later you'll be surprised to realize that there will no longer be any need for a team time log.

7 IMPORTANT TIPS TO MANAGE TIME WISELY DURING A MEETING

When it comes to managing time within a team, one of the most crucial areas that you need to pay attention to is how you handle a meeting. Planning and conducting meetings can be very time-consuming so you have to learn how to do these things effectively without wasting your time and the time of the group members.

Here are 5 important tips that you can apply for effective team time management during a meeting:

Plan Ahead.
Never, ever conduct a meeting without planning ahead. When you don't have a clear agenda prepared, there is no specific direction. You'll end up going different ways and bringing up various topics and concerns that may not be significant at the moment. At the end, you might not be able to achieve your desired results if you have no set goals for the outcome of the meeting.

When planning for a meeting, make sure to take note of who should be there and what each would contribute. This way, you can avoid wasting other people's time too if they are not really needed for a particular meeting. Plan the specific objectives too and the inclusions in the agenda that would best help the group attain the anticipated and preferred results.

Start on Time.
As much as possible, you should always start on time. Even if there are group members who are not yet present, don't make it a habit to wait for them or they will never make an effort in the future to come on time. Of course you ought to inform them also beforehand that the meeting will begin on time so it is of utmost importance for them to be there early or on the dot.

One effective method to encourage people to come on time for meetings is to come up with a type of penalty that everybody agrees on. This can be a late fee, buying snacks for the group, or taking on an additional responsibility or task.

Begin with the Objectives.
In order to ensure that everyone is on the same page from the very beginning of the meeting, you have to state the objectives before anything else. What do you intend to discuss and accomplish within the given time? This has to be well-defined but should also be realistic. Make a checklist that you can go back to before closing the meeting.

Evaluate Previous Meeting.
Don't forget to evaluate the previous meeting before proceeding. Go back to the things you were supposed to complete then but were not able to realize. Assess the reasons why and make it a goal to avoid such for the present meeting.

Set the Ground Rules.
Also establish your ground rules that would help in excellent team time management during the meeting. These can include timing presentations, maintaining focus and avoiding topic deviations, and showing respect for the ones who are speaking or sharing.

Maintain Good Communication.
Even if you are trying to manage time wisely, it's still very im-

portant to give each person the chance to speak their mind and to share their views. As the facilitator of the meeting, it is your job to encourage the articulation of relevant concerns as well as the expression of opinions about the topic being discussed. Remember that good communication within the group and among the members is highly essential for remarkable team dynamics that will also contribute greatly to outstanding team time management.

Summarize and Analyze.
Before officially closing the meeting, you should summarize the action plans that came out of the discussion. What tasks have to be done and who are in charge? Go over your delegation sheet. Set clear time frames as well.

Furthermore, you also need to analyze the meeting itself. This is the time to bring out your checklist of objectives and to note down which ones were not accomplished and why. You also have to briefly confer with the group how you can further improve the meeting next time. And of course, don't forget to set the date and time (ideally the venue too) for the next meeting.

Make sure to congratulate everyone once again for a good meeting and recognize those who were able to get their assigned tasks done on time. Highlight the good points of the team but also motivate the people to do better in the areas for improvement.

With these beneficial tips for managing time wisely during a meeting, you'll surely end up accomplishing much more and thus having more reason and time to celebrate as a team.

MAKE TIME YOUR SUPERHERO POWER!

CHAPTER TWELVE: WRITTEN COMMUNICATION

"When topics are complex and meaty, don't create a never-ending email thread. It's amazing how much time people waste composing and reading carefully-worded essays, when a 5 minute in-person chat would resolve the whole thing."

JUSTIN ROSENSTEIN

OVERVIEW

Written communication, whether it's paper or digital, is a crucial medium for most businesses and organizations. However, if it's not managed and systematized properly, it can create overwhelming levels of clutter and ultimately waste a tremendous amount of time. Learning to optimize the written communications that are necessary for your work – as well as learning to eliminate those that are redundant or avoidable – is a central aspect of time management.

HOW CLUTTER CLOUDS OVER EFFECTIVE COMMUNICATION IN THE WORKPLACE

Have you ever experienced looking at the piles of paper on your desk and just wanting to slump back in your chair and give up? Have you ever checked your e-mail inbox and felt overwhelmed with confusion as to which one to attend to first? Both electronic and written communication cannot be avoided in the workplace, and have the tendency to engulf and crush you when they grow at a faster rate than you can handle. Indeed, this overload will sometimes freeze you in place or stress you out so much that you'll likely become far less productive.

What is the Clutter Law?
In the corporate world and in other fields of work, there is such a thing known as the "Clutter Law." This law states that clutter has the natural tendency to keep on expanding when there is available space. Clutter always fills up the available space. Hence, you

have to be constantly standing guard and staying on top of it.

How Does Clutter Affect Communication?

Yes, it can be very challenging to clear the workplace of written communication in various forms. These days, it's even more difficult to monitor and limit the electronic communication flooding your e-mail and social media accounts. When this happens and you are unable to handle it, clutter will surely overpower you and result in confusion and poor productivity.

Clutter cannot be ignored, because it will keep on piling up and affecting communication. Some memos may get lost in the mound of papers. You may tend to lose track of your files and documents. You may mix up important papers too. You will get to develop poor work habits if you are always surrounded with clutter and you do not do anything about it.

How Can You Handle Communication Overload Better?

If you are in the position to minimize files, documents, and paper work, you should do so. Perhaps you can send e-mails instead of written documents. There are times when you can make do with paperless work. If you feel as if you're not in the position, you can suggest this to your superior. Make sure to provide sufficient supporting reasons and examples.

You should also come up with a simple system to sort all your written communications as they come to you. Set aside time each day to attend to this task, so that you will not have to worry about piling up files and papers. Make use of folders, filing cabinets, and the like and be sure to label each one. Also allot a few hours each week or every other week to remove old papers that you don't need to keep anymore.

When it comes to electronic communication, it's best to make sure that you have a separate email account to use for work purposes and one for personal matters. This way, you will not have to be bothered with work when you are at home or on vacation. You can also save time while browsing through work email when there are no other emails inserted into your inbox. This is also one way to avoid distractions while in the office or during your work hours.

Applying these simple recommendations will help you avoid clutter and thus also facilitate better communication in the workplace.

WRITTEN COMMUNICATIONS: A HABIT TO BE CORRECTED

For the longest time, it seems as if different forms of written communication have been going around in offices and organizations in tremendous volumes. Even with modern technology today, although many institutions have gone "paperless," it's only a simple transition from paper to electronic memos and documents. Nevertheless, the overwhelming amount remains the same.

A Bad Habit
It has become a habit for different organizations to make use of written communications not only to keep in touch and remind people of different things, but to also monitor progress and be constantly reminded about what has to be done or completed. It is thus considered a bad habit that needs to be corrected.

Many believe that often associated with the development and propagation of this habit is the fact that documents and paperwork are deemed an end instead of just being means to the real end. These are the tangible things that office workers and even managers hold on to just to feel as if they are moving forward and getting a lot accomplished.

Take a look at your current situation, wherever you are working. If you're in this boat, it's time for a turnaround. You need to break this bad habit.

Breaking the Habit

The bad habit of excessive written communications has to be broken and directed to something healthier and more productive. Perhaps there are several memos and documents that are not really necessary. Maybe you can lessen the paperwork, especially if some seem redundant. This is a great challenge for many people. But in the same way that the habit came about, you can also work on making it a habit to have less written communications or to limit these to the more important concerns and only those that are necessary.

Begin slowly. Begin with yourself. Go over your files and take out those that have been sitting there for years but are not needed anymore. Check your email inbox and also review your sent items to have a clearer idea of which appear to be taking up a lot of your time and seemingly keeping you busy but you can already do without.

Next, move on to your own team. If you're in the position to impose paperwork, make sure to consult with the members of the team so that together you can all decide on which ones you can trash and which you believe should be continued. Surely there are some forms of communication that you can already do without and may even give you more time for other, more essential items.

One way you can evaluate what ought to be kept or continued is to determine which documents actually bring about results and help you and the team move toward your goals. You might be surprised to discover that there is plenty of paperwork you waste your time on that doesn't really help much in the long run but simply appears to be important on the surface.

Certainly, the humongous bulk of written communications that piles up on your desk and in your computer can be avoided and prevented in a constructive way that will benefit you and your work enormously.

4 WAYS TO HANDLE YOUR WRITTEN COMMUNICATIONS AT WORK

If you wish to take charge of your time and deal with it more efficiently, you need to learn how to handle your written communications at work. Whether you work in the office or out in the field, you're a freelancer, or you have your own business, you really have to live with both paper and electronic documents every single day. Most of the time, these forms of written communication can take up a lot of time that should have been used up for more productive things. Hence, it's vital for you to handle them well.

Deciding to Dump
Which written communications do you often dump? Some people read a memo that does not apply to them or does not have much bearing, and then throw them straight in the trash. Others see promotional emails and delete them immediately. There are those who decide to dump bills in the garbage in order to avoid worrying about them. Of course this last example is certainly not advisable. Bills will not go away if you dump them, but will

get even worse.

You must be aware of your priorities and be able to tell what's important from what is not. For instance, if you receive minutes of the last meeting you attended or the progress report of your subordinate, you can't just dump these. But if you get a flyer for a product you're not interested in or a notice about the new canteen food, then you can certainly throw them away.

Learning to Delegate
One of the better ways to save time when it comes to written communications is to delegate some of them for other people to handle. You can do this if you have a secretary or if you have your own team or department. Of course you must also determine which ones suit their job descriptions and also those that they can handle. If there's a decision to be made, for instance, on a proposal sent, it may be that you are the best person to handle it. Then this document is something you cannot delegate.

Doing the Job
Of course, an obvious way to handle written communications is to just do what is expected or asked. For example, the document may need to be forwarded to the entire team or properly filed. If you find it important, then go and do it. Don't set it aside as you may forget to do it later on. Perhaps you can place it in your folder of documents to be filed so that you can attend to it during your scheduled filing period.

What's essential here is for you to remember that you do not need to act on everything that you receive. There is some paperwork that you ought to delegate or just throw away.

Delaying the Process
Many individuals delay the process of attending to the written communications they receive. Sometimes it's because they are too busy with other tasks and activities. Other times there are those who choose to just ignore it for the moment. Often, delaying will result in piled up work that will surely waste your time. It can also lead to missed deadlines and poor performance. Al-

though this is a common way that a lot of people deal with paper and electronic documents, you should always avoid picking this path to follow.

The first three alternatives discussed above are all acceptable and recommended, provided that you're able to discern which documents ought to be dumped, delegated, and/or done. The last alternative, delaying, will almost always lead to problems, so this is what you should stay away from even if it is the most tempting.

HOW TO HAVE A CLEANING OUT PARTY

Because written communications often result in overflowing drawers and folders, plenty of unread emails, and lots of wasted time, you need to have a cleaning out party every now and then. Ideally, this has to be done two to four times a year so you can effectively handle the influx of written communications and be able to maintain an orderly and clean workplace.

Scheduling
It's best to schedule your cleaning out party every end of the quarter or every six months. Don't do it just when you feel like it, because sorting papers and even electronic documents takes up a lot of time and may get in the way of your other tasks and activities. Hence you need to allot several hours for it on a day when you know you won't be as busy or there are no major projects that need your focus.

Planning
Just like with a real party, planning is essential. Aside from setting the schedule, you must also prepare folders and boxes for all those you may need to file. You should also plan for the ones you intend to delegate: Which ones will go to whom? Where will you place those for filing? Which ones have to be thrown out per-

manently? Perhaps you have so many documents that you may need help managing everything. You might also need markers to label the boxes or trash bags to collect papers for dumping.

Implementing

The actual implementation of the cleaning out part is the most difficult. It's very time-consuming and can be energy-draining too. Why don't you turn it into a fun event by doing it together with friends or colleagues? If you are a team leader, make it a bonding activity for your team and come up with mini contests wherein prizes will be given away. You can even inject a treasure hunt. This way, people's energies will be up instead of down.

Before implementing your plans, make sure a clear system has been laid out so that you don't end up throwing away some essential documents or looking for papers later on that you have misplaced.

Celebrating

Naturally, you ought not to forget the celebrating part. Even if you do the sorting and cleaning all by yourself, completing the task calls for some reward that will make you feel good about it and will encourage you to keep on doing it in the future. If you're with a group, all the more reason to celebrate! Go out for snacks and drinks afterward so that you can relax together and have real fun.

Celebrating puts people in a great mood and will make them feel that accomplishing the cleaning out party is truly important.

When you follow the steps described above, you'll surely have successful cleaning out parties. As a result, you can stop worrying and wasting time over the growing amount of written communications in your work.

CONCLUSION

"Lack of direction, not lack of time, is the problem. We all have twenty-four hour days."

ZIG ZIGLAR

YOUR SUPERHERO POWER

Just like Superman has a constellation of abilities -- from x-ray vision to flying -- that make him who he is, there are a constellation of abilities -- from analyzing to written communication -- that will make time your superhero power.
This book has outlined many strategies and systems and now it's time to put this new knowledge to use.

Integrating these principles and strategies into your day-to-day life is the hard part, but once you accomplish it, you'll find that it was well worth your while. You can look forward to reduced stress levels, increased productivity and efficiency, a higher quality of work, and more time to spend as you please. Your career outlook, home life and overall personal happiness all stand to benefit from your newly acquired time management skills.

There is no denying that it will be a struggle at first, as you redefine and improve upon deeply-entrenched habits and routines.

Some steps will be obvious – for example, reducing your time spent on activities that you've always known to drain your time, like social media – but that doesn't necessarily mean that they will be easy to complete. Take each process at your own pace and remember to personalize the approach according to your own specific needs, strengths and ultimate goals.

ABOUT SCOTT GRAHAM

Scott is a business and career coach from Boston, MA. When he is not coaching people to be their best, he participates in Tough Mudders, hikes, works on a farm, practices Vipassana meditation, or volunteers as an EMT and firefighter.

BOOKS BY SCOTT GRAHAM

Ten Things You Need to Know About Coaching Before You Get a Coach

Motivational Interviewing Made Easy

Work Exchange: A Handbook for Hosts

How to Become More Linkable… …and Likeable on LinkedIn

Check! Your Guide to Creating a Life Transforming Bucket List

Growing & Using Good King Henry

Make Time Your Superhero Power!

Get Off Your Ass & Mow The Grass!

Now what? After Your Vipassana Course Is Over

Determining Marijuana Use in the Age of Legalization

Androphile Pride

Treatment Planning 101

Come As You Are: Meditation & Grief

CONTACT SCOTT GRAHAM

True Azimuth, LLC
265 Franklin Street
Suite 1702
Boston, MA 02110

Phone: (617) 475-0081

Website: http://TrueAzimuth.biz

Email: sgraham@TrueAzimuth.biz

Skype: TrueAzimuth

Twitter: @TrueAzimuth

Goodreads: https://www.goodreads.com/grahamgscott

Facebook: http://www.facebook.com/trueazimuthcoaching

Google+: http://plus.google.com/+TrueazimuthBiz-BusinessCoach

LinkedIn: http://www.linkedin.com/company/true-azimuth-llc

www.ingramcontent.com/pod-product-compliance
Lightning Source LLC
Chambersburg PA
CBHW060832220526
45466CB00003B/1074